Less Stress, More Joy

The Peace, Harmony, Joy Approach

Scott Frank

Yossi Lerman

This book is for informational purposes only. It is not intended to provide medical advice and should not be relied on for such. The authors do not guarantee or warrant that the information in this book is accurate, complete, or up-to-date. This information is general in nature and may not apply to particular circumstances. This book does not create a doctor-patient relationship between you and the authors. This book is not a substitute for sound judgment, and you should not act upon any of the information in this book without first confirming that the suggestions, processes and information in this book are appropriate for your situation. Please consult a doctor for medical advice.

Less Stress, More Joy: The Peace, Harmony, Joy Approach

Scott's Dedication

This book is dedicated to my family. I have been blessed with an amazing wife, Marie, who is always there to support me and share incredible life experiences with. My four children, Dennis, Danielle, David and Diana, are all gifts from G-d and have taught me a lot about life. I also appreciate my parents, Denny and Ellen, who gave me the strong foundation for helping people, confidence to make a difference, and love of family. Special thanks to my siblings, Brian and Marcy, for their encouragement and lifelong memories.

Yossi's Dedication

I dedicate this book (and my life) to the mission outlined by the Rebbe, Rabbi Menachem M. Schneerson, to make the world a better place, a brighter place, a cleaner place, a peaceful place, and a holier place one person at a time, one thought at a time, and one word at a time. Our mission is clear: give people hope and purpose, give people a better understanding of the essence of LIFE, and give people a rock-solid foundation to walk on. I thank my wonderful family for educating and supporting me with unconditional love and sensitivity.

NOTE: Throughout the book, the authors have decided to use the word G-d as another word for God. And G-d is intended to mean the *Creator*, the *Divine*, and the *Source* of all being for those who believe in G-d

TABLE OF CONTENTS

Foreword by Les Brown

If today was all you had, what would it be like? Heck, if this moment is actually the only one you have, will you be able to look retrospectively and say, you have had peaceful, harmonious, and joyous relationships and life? The vast majority of us will answer in the negative! Yet, we are in pursuit of peace, harmony, and joy in every facet of our lives. Many do not have the tools, or the commitment to attain this lofty, yet elusive ideal. Now, there is the book you are holding in your hands, *Less Stress, More Joy – The Peace, Harmony, Joy Approach* by Scott Frank and Yossi Lerman, to fill this void.

In my over five decades of being involved in personal development, self-help, life, and professional coaching, and as a motivational speaker, I have read and authored several books. I have also been to a plethora of workshops, trainings, and seminars. If it is a book on self-help out there, I have just about read it all. In my various capacities, I have interacted with all sorts of people, and one thing I have found is that a common thread weaves through most, if not all. There is the yearning for a better life and future. We all want to live peacefully, harmoniously, and joyfully. The question has always been how? Not why, when, or where? But how? Now, this book provides answers and tools to this nagging question. Few books, if any, have had the sort of impact this book has had on me. In fact, I am on my fifth go around of reading it. Seven being my lucky number almost guarantees that I will be reading it for a seventh time, and it will definitely be within my reach to consult.

The fact is, Less Stress, More Joy is not just a casual read. Rather it is a study that offers practical hands-on approaches that should be a constant companion until the principles articulated are mastered. The principles and approaches presented are simple, concise, and powerful. They are to-the-point practical principles that when committed to will undoubtedly lead to a self-aware, peaceful, harmonious, and joyous self. This in turn, will ultimately translate into peaceful, harmonious, and joyous co-existence between you, your family, your peers, and colleagues. This is a once-in-a-generation kind of book. It is a game-changer!

With global anxiety at an all-time high due to the pandemic, the economical fallouts from it, and the U.S. being in such a historically polarized quagmire, there is no better time than now for such a book to help cope. This is especially true with us being inundated with a deluge of information, social media and other distractions that shift our anchors. Sadly, suicides are at an all-time high, and so are divorces and family breakdowns. These are dire times. But we must remain hopeful that this too shall pass. It is my candid belief that this status-quo has presented all of us with unprecedented opportunities. There is no better time than now to hit the pause button and take individual and collective stock. It is incumbent on each person to ask of themselves objectively and subjectively how they are managing their emotions, their physical and spiritual wellbeing, and their interactions with the world around them. This is a time for personal *"look-in-the-mirror"* assessment moment. The uncertainties about the pandemic and the abject lack of cooperative governance which has exacerbated the polarization further illustrates that we are at a major intersection. How we proceed will have generational consequences. The sort of legacies and futures we leave behind for our children and families bears directly upon the choices and decisions we make individually and collectively. No doubt, in order to succeed at making a positive impact, the right tools are indeed necessary. And so are the willing and dedicated persons to carry this on. "Less Stress, More Joy—The Peace, Harmony and Joy Approach" is precisely what the proverbial doctor ordered! With the tools provided by Scott Frank and Yossi Lerman, there is hope—an ingredient in desperate need. Without hope there can be nothing but doom!

As a template, the Peace, Harmony and Joy Approach emphasizes gratitude, humility, relationship capital, self-worth, effective communication, and respect for the dignity of everyone, including individual dignity. It further illuminates that, how we treat our bodies aligns proportionately with our value systems, outlooks and ultimately, our lives. What a concept? This easy, yet compelling book is a must read for any and everyone who is serious about living a meaningful, purposeful, and tranquil life. While both Scott and Yossi have not promised an elixir or some sort of utopic existence, they offer practical approaches to help deal with those moments that can derail our peace, harmony, and joy.

I have had the privilege of knowing both Scott and Yossi for some time now, and they both exemplify the "Peace, Harmony and Joy" approach. They live and breathe these principles. Their commitment to this way of life is undeniable and infectious. They are indeed true ambassadors of these principles. It is no surprise Scott translates these virtues in his professional life as an effective and pleasant leader at a fortune 10 company, as well as other successful ventures he is undertaking. Yossi on the other hand, is equally magnanimous, and quite the magnetic personality. Because of this, Yossi has a legion of ardent followers, one of whom is very dear to me. His community continues to grow because of his principled approach and dynamism. I have personally been impacted by both Scott and Yossi.

As someone who has made a career and life of helping people alter the false narratives of themselves, and shift their stalled professional lives, I know a thing or two, because I have seen a thing or two. Anyone committed to the promise of our future and the quality of life our progenitors will inherit will undoubtedly invest in diligently studying and inculcating the PHJ principles succinctly and lucidly laid out in this book: "Less Stress, More Joy—the Peace, Harmony and Joy Approach". This is my story, and I am sticking to it!

You are something special, you have greatness within you. But you've got to be Hungry! This has been Mrs. Mamie Brown's Baby Boy, and Dorothy Rucker's Pride and Joy, challenging everyone to live peacefully, harmoniously, and joyously the Scott and Yossi way. Take the challenge!

Foreword by Dianne Collins with Alan K. Collins

What lasts forever are the universal truths—the sparks of wisdom that ignite the heart and soothe the soul. What persists is the yearning for these truths, particularly when it feels as though the experience of them is lacking.

Peace. Harmony. Joy. These are three of the truths of which we speak and the noble focus of authors, Scott Frank and Yossi Lerman. These are qualities of being that every one of us longs for. Many of us go through life in pursuit of those experiences as goals to reach.

Yet, there is a deeper truth that can resolve what has seemed to elude us since time immemorial. That deeper truth is this: Peace, Harmony and Joy are the foundation of *who we are*. These qualities of being form the essence of who we are, both as individuals and as the collective core of humanity.

Then why, one rightly asks—why does it seem so far from our actual experience? Why don't we consistently experience Peace, Harmony and Joy in ourselves, in our families and in our larger communities?

What is missing, the discovery of which would resolve the looming problems of divisiveness and conflict, confusion and hopelessness that fill the airwaves of modern culture? Is there an answer, a solution, a holy grail to be found, once and for all—that all peoples live in a golden age now and forever? As QuantumThinkers, we know the answer to this question is a resounding YES! The QuantumThink® wisdom is that we are co-creators in a reality of Infinite Possibility. The authors of this precious book, Scott Frank and Yossi Lerman, also know this to be true, and desire that every person feels the impeccable truth of it in their hearts.

Scott Frank is the embodiment of greatness intertwined with graciousness. He not only thinks big and with boundless possibility; he acts. He gets it done. He manifests results that didn't seem possible. He inspires others to do the same. To know that they can. And they do.

We met Scott in a different context, as a world renowned highly respected leader in Intellectual Property. We have had the privilege of working with him and his leadership team applying Strategic QuantumThink® Consulting to their business. QuantumThink is a methodology for thinking. You look from the whole and for the whole of any situation, with the express purpose to benefit all. You view life from the Perspective of All Perspectives, moving beyond automatic conditioned beliefs and assumptions and break free of limiting thoughts. You think and live from Infinite Possibility. You realize the power of your very own mind. You consciously master the creative dynamic of Intent. Scott immediately resonated with these principles, recognizing them as keys to achieving our highest aspirations.

Yossi Lerman is gentle soul with a powerful presence you feel in every moment of being with him. He exudes the wisdom of heart and soul from every fiber of his being. In Yossi we encounter a rarity—the purity of an authentic spiritual leader infused with the humility of an ordinary person with the courage to continuously do self-inquiry—that he may live the virtues of our divine nature. With the support and guidance of faith, he is his own checkpoint that maintains his clarity and focus.

The Divinely destined joining together of these two extraordinary individuals is a gift to all of us. Their vision is clear: that every creature of life experiences the foundation of their being as peaceful, harmonious and joyful. That the world is a veritable vortex of Peace, Harmony and Joy we are happily swept up into.

From such an unshakable foundation, whatever unfolds in daily life in both our personal and shared worlds, is indubitably imbued with the spirit of these universal truths.

Scott Frank and Yossi Lerman are not merely authors who wish to impart an inspiring philosophy. They are great souls who have taken on a huge mission tantamount to a literal quantum leap for humankind. As you read *Less Stress, More Joy* you experience it as a treasure connecting you to your true essence. You become a force in awakening this vital awareness. *Peace, Harmony and Joy* are alive in you, and you know it.

Dianne Collins, Creator of QuantumThink® with
Alan K. Collins, Master QuantumThink® Coach

Acknowledgements

We wish to acknowledge a lot of people who have helped us with this book. Thank you to Fran Redisch for inputting our hard to read, handwritten draft and revising it many times, and Marie Frank, Scott's wife, for revising the final versions. We appreciate the suggested revisions and ideas of Dennis Frank, Dianne Collins, Alan Collins, Andy Heller, Marcy Saucedo, Lisa Lai, Kevin Cranman, Jane Mudgett, Dalila Rosenstrauch, Danielle Frank and Jamie Ellickson. We also give special thanks to those who have participated in our PHJ workshops to help us develop our thinking, including Shelly Katzef, Robin Joseph, Arthur Levin, Fran Redisch, Sam Kaplan, Israel Ben-Eliezer, Dan Siegel, Susan Siegel, Alex Gilelach, Vanessa Gilelach, Paul Mears, Nancy Mears, Esther Lerman, Shaina Lerman, Marie Frank, Ellen Frank and Peter Klokow. A very special thanks to Mary Saucedo for her beautifully designed book cover and Barry Brager for the smartly-designed website: www.peaceharmonyjoy.org. Finally, the ultimate thanks goes to G-d for giving us the strength, wisdom, and confidence to put our thoughts to writing and sharing them with you.

INTRODUCTION

Today we live in a world that can easily be high stress. Every day the news reports on unpleasant occurrences happening all around us. The smart phone and our laptop computer keep us connected to the world, our friends, family, and jobs like a leash no matter where we go. Social media makes it quick and easy to feel like we are comparing and competing, left out, or put down. The responsibilities as a parent, spouse, and employee continue to mount. The cost of homes, cars, and vacations seem never ending. Even for children, there seems to be more homework, after school activities, and more peer pressure than ever.

With all of these stresses, it is not surprising that many are simply resigned to surviving each day. These people may take to drinking, drugs, eating, binge watching, and other bad habits to escape their realities. However, this form of stress reduction turns out to be temporary and often adds to one's stress over time. Is it any wonder that people living like this are not experiencing much Joy in their lives? Even when they have moments of Joy it is short lived and fleeting. Many may not even remember what Joy is or feels like.

So what is Joy? Joy is a wonderful feeling. It is more than being happy and having a good time. Good food, weekends and vacations make us happy. However, they rarely bring people Joy in and of themselves. After all, Joy is more than something that makes you feel good or gives you pleasure. Joy, as we talk about it, is a state of well-being and bliss. Joy is a positive, healthy state of mind, a feeling that makes your being feel energized, invigorated, elevated, strong, and fully alive. We are not just existing . . . we're living!

For many, Joy is one's ultimate connection with G-d. Those times when everything feels just right, and we feel G-d's strong presence. By being in a state of Joy, we are pleasing to G-d and the whole world, showing our love and appreciation for all He has provided and for the people in our life. It is a place of spiritual and emotional enlightenment. "Jumping for Joy" is an old saying, and can also be thought of as the feeling of getting even closer to G-d.

While we are blessed with many talents and strengths, their full power often remains dormant. Joy is an opener. It unleashes our potential and drives our strengths and energy to flow outward and upward. Joy is a liberating, Exodus experience. It frees the mind and body to achieve new heights, to operate at 100% peak performance. Joy has the power to break all walls, obstacles, and barriers more than muscles and hard work can accomplish. Joy helps us in areas like ingenious thinking and problem-solving, and Joy positions us for true success in life and self-mastery.

Who wouldn't want more of this Joyful feeling within one's self and with others? Why don't more people feel Joy consistently every month, every week, every day or even all day? Where can you find it? When can you most expect it? What are ways to increase the likelihood of it?

Wouldn't you want to feel less anger, less fear, less worry, less sadness, and less anxiety? Those toxic emotions that weaken, rob, and drain your life's light and energy. Is life all about work, work.. busy, busy... stress and more pressure? How do you break free from this vicious cycle? How can you gain control back into your life?

We, Scott and Yossi, have been asking ourselves these questions for much of our lives. While we may not have always asked the same exact questions, we both have been in search of our best lives for many years, and Joy has been central to it. Both of us have come at it with life lessons from experiences, self help books, conferences, and coaching. Though he believes deeply in G-d, Scott's reading has been mostly "non-religious" literature, such as *Do You QuantumThink?*, *The Mindbody Prescription*, and *Discover Your Destiny*. On the other hand, Yossi's has been "deeply religious", often from intense studies of the *Torah*, *Talmud* and *Tanya*.

When we first began discussing the topic of Joy in 2013, we both realized that we had been searching for the same thing with two different treasure maps. We also realized that neither of us had all of the answers, and both of us had a lot of theories developed through significant time and thinking. We both also observed that by coming at Joy with deep religious and non-religious learnings, we may be able to discover a new approach helpful to us and others. What follows is the culmination of significant time, research, and conversations, including many workshops, about what we believe is a unique approach to reducing one's stress and bringing more Joy into one's life.

We believe less stress and more Joy is a choice you make. It doesn't depend on what you have in your possession, where you live, or what you look like. Less stress and more Joy is a skill that can be learned. The essential factor is based on your attitude and mindset towards life, towards yourself, towards other people, towards events, and towards situations.

We also believe that G-d gave each of us a beautiful temple encompassed in our body, mind, and soul. He has given us everything we need for an amazing and Joyful life. It is up to us to make the most of what we have and discover ways to live a less stressful and more Joyful life.

Whether you're by yourself, with your family, at work, playing sports, or at a community event, we believe the approach and related techniques we've discovered will significantly reduce the stress and positively impact the Joy you experience every day. We wish you the best as you join us on this Joyful Journey!

START BY CHECKING YOUR OWN POCKETS

Reb Mendel Futerfas was one of the outstanding heroes who survived Stalin's Gulag prisons in Siberia. After many years of forced labor as punishment for his "crime" of helping strengthen Jewish life in the Soviet Union, he was eventually able to leave Russia and reunite in London with his wife, who had also escaped Russia years earlier. Often he would sit with friends and students, and recall his prison experiences and the lessons that he learned from them.

One of the activities prohibited in the Gulag was playing cards. It was considered a severe crime, and harsh punishment was imposed on one caught violating this prison rule. Somehow though, the inmates managed to smuggle in a deck of cards and would while away their free time with the forbidden game. The guards were told about the breach and came to inspect the prisoners' quarters. They found nothing. As weeks went by and the games continued, the guards were baffled. "Are these uncouth prisoners outsmarting us?" they wondered. They finally decided to put an end to this affront on their authority and pride and carried out a surprise inspection, checking every inch of the barracks as well as the bodies and clothes of all inmates. They found nothing. They came to the conclusion that the informer had lied to them, either to curry favor in their eyes or to make a joke out of them.

As soon as the inspectors left, the cards appeared and the games continued as usual. Reb Mendel couldn't understand how it had happened. The inspectors had checked every possible hiding place. Eventually he was let in on the secret. "You see," the head inmate began, "many in here are professional pickpockets. As soon as the guards would enter the barracks, the pickpockets would slip the cards into guards' pockets. Right before they would leave, the pickpockets would slip them back out again. Obviously, it never occurred to the guards to check their own pockets."

The lesson is clear. If you want to make an accurate assessment of reality, start your search by checking your own pockets. Often, when we take our spiritual and personal inventory, we instinctively look to place blame on those around us. "My parents are responsible", "my wife is responsible", "my education is responsible", etc. Everyone is blamed except oneself. That is an easier and less painful way to do things, but it is not effective in the long run. If you really want to put your life in order, you must not overlook your own "pockets."

Remember:

Every time you point a finger at someone else, you have three fingers pointing back at yourself!

THE PEACE, HARMONY, JOY APPROACH.

From all of our learnings and conversations, we believe there are two key states one should have in their life to position themselves consistently for less stress and more JOY.

PEACE and HARMONY

Why Peace?

So how does Peace play into this? Well, Peace is essentially the opposite of stress, whether it is stress within your body, stress in your relationships, or stress in your community. If you want to have less stress in your life, you need to live life on the other end of the spectrum called Peace. In addition, it is difficult to have consistent Joy when you don't have inner Peace-of-mind, tranquility, and calm within yourself, within your family, and within your community.

When we do not have Peace within ourselves, we feel anxious and annoyed. These feelings pretty much zap most of our energy and our chances of feeling Joy. Being pulled in all directions, worried, overwhelmed, overloaded, and having too many balls to juggle can all cause our body to suffer headaches, backaches, and stomachaches. At times like this, it is hard for our mind to be in the moment and enjoy what is happening at the

15

present. It is hard to find Joy in almost anything when you feel confused and panicky. Peace and serenity within ourselves are essential for feeling more Joy.

When we do not have Peace within our families, we have a lot of arguing, fighting, and holding grudges. The family members don't feel comfortable with each other, they worry about the next fight or bad surprise, and trust is lacking. It is hard to find Joy in the family relationship when this occurs. Therefore, we need to find ways to have more Peaceful times within our families. In this book we teach ways to have more respect for each family member, be more thoughtful with words and actions toward each other, and reduce the verbal, psychological, and physical pain for more Peaceful and Joyful family experiences.

When we do not have Peace within our communities, we team up against each other and make others uncomfortable. We use verbal and written communications to hurt others who look different or have opposing opinions. Sometimes this leads to riots or even wars. It is hard to find Joy in the community when this takes place. When we have Peace within our communities, people of different ethnic backgrounds, religions, genders and opinions get along, respect each other, and do not cause harm to others leading to a more Joyful place.

Why Harmony?

So if you have consistent Peace in your life, are you likely to have less stress and more consistent Joy? Maybe on the stress, but not likely on the Joy. This is because while more Peace will directly reduce your stress level, in most cases Harmony is needed to bridge Peace and Joy.

The opposite of Harmony is confusion and chaos. It is hard to imagine less stress and more Joy in confused and chaotic moments. Yet many feel this unpleasant emotional state many times throughout their week and even every day.

Harmony problems within ourselves often occur when we try to live a life that others want us to live as opposed to living the life that we want. It may be your parents, friends, or spouse. I would like to have this career, try this hobby, or explore this talent, but others tell me not to.

Do you find yourself living many different and sometimes diverse lives and may be torn apart between your work and family time, moral code and pleasurable temptations, ethical values and making the deal, spiritual and physical needs, and mind and heart?

On the other hand, Harmony within occurs when you take your G-d-given talents, gifts, passions, and interests and make the most of them in a united single force. It occurs when your body, mind, and heart work together as one whole person towards a single purpose and goal so that whatever you're doing feels natural and flows well. You see and feel the oneness in yourself.

Harmony within yourself happens when you see life as a rainbow, hear the amazing music your body emanates, and feel the beautiful beat of life. You feel confident and comfortable being fully yourself and doing the things you truly enjoy for a more Harmonious and Joyful life.

Lack of Harmony within a family occurs when each member is not on the same page. One tries to share their perspective and gets shut down by another. Judgments, assumptions and speculations are the norm. People stop talking and listening to each other. A family member wants to participate in a family project, but the others don't want them to do what they like or are good at doing. Similar dynamics can take place in organizations, such as work, team sports, and community groups.

Harmony within your family occurs when each family member appreciates and respects the others' unique talents and gifts given to them by G-d. It occurs when each family member is able to use these talents and gifts in a complementary, interwoven fashion to make the family better, stronger, and more fun. Harmony within the family happens when each one's different personalities, perspectives, and approaches are brought together in a collaborative manner to achieve great outcomes.

Lack of Harmony in communities occurs when people stereotype, don't take the time to get to know their neighbors, have a hard time putting themselves in others' shoes, and draw incorrect conclusions and biases about others around them. Groups of people then feel left out, mistreated, and hurt.

Harmony within our communities occurs when people appreciate each other's different backgrounds, religions, genders, and more. It occurs when people understand that these differences and diversity make the community stronger and better. When Harmony within the community happens, people feel comfortable being themselves and coming together with others for wonderful and Joy filled times.

Harmony is what makes life full and wonderful. It happens when we are sharing our best with the world. When this occurs, we have our best interactions with others and make amazing music together.

The Interrelationship of Peace, Harmony, and Joy

You now understand what we mean by Peace, Harmony, and Joy. You would also agree that it would be great to have each of them in our life on a consistent basis, especially for consistent Joy in our lives. So how do they relate to each other and why do you need them to occur in the order of Peace... Harmony...Joy?

Peace is the Foundation

We believe that Joy in one's life often starts with inner Peace. In addition, we believe it is hard, if not impossible, to have consistent Joy in your family and community without consistent Peace in each one.

If you are feeling internal anxiety and stress, you are pretty much not able to live a Joyful life. It is hard to find much Joy in anything. If you're consistently fighting with your family members, it is difficult to find Joy with them. If your community is filled with tension and hatred, it will be challenging to find Joy there.

On the other hand, when you feel inner tranquility and calm, your body and mind are now positioned to experience Joy. If you are on good terms with your family and there is a mutual respect, then you are now more likely to experience Joy with them. If your community has good relations and people are civil to each other, there is more likely to be Joy in community events.

While we believe Peace is the foundation that is often necessary for consistent Joy in your life, your family, and your community, there is still a void between the two. Yes, Peace creates the opportunity, yet something must occur to position the Joy.

Harmony is the Bridge

This is where Harmony comes in. Peace is like the white canvas, and Harmony is like the colored paints to create a masterpiece. Peace is like a salad bowl, and the elegantly mixed ingredients are the Harmony. Peace is like the orchestra stage, and Harmony the talented musicians that perform well together during a concert.

When your mind is at Peace it can pull together thoughts from different parts of the brain in Harmony to create wonderful visions and artwork. When the body is at Peace, it can coordinate the different body parts and muscles to perform great athletic feats and musical performances. When the heart is at Peace, it can lovingly guide and push the mind and body in Harmony to places of love and care for others. When the mind, body and heart are all at Peace and in Harmony, they can create Oscar-winning performances, set Olympic records, and master once-in-a-lifetime achievements.

When the family is at Peace, it can come together in Harmony to create beautiful dinners, outings, vacations, game playing, and conversations. When the community is at Peace, it can come together in Harmony to cheer for their favorite team, help those in need, and share in special events.

All of these Harmony moments are able to consistently occur when we have Peace. They are also a result of you, your family, and your community, making the most of your and their talents, gifts, passions, and interests.

Joy is the Culmination

While we believe that Peace creates the opportunity for Harmony that can lead to Joy, it does not guarantee it. Just because you create a masterpiece or set an Olympic record does not mean you are certain to experience Joy. In the same light, a beautiful family dinner or fun family vacation does not guarantee Joy, nor does the community cheering on its favorite team to victory or the community having a beautiful parade.

There are many athletes, and even Olympians, who have had moments of greatness and even set world records, yet do not even remember much of the experience. Where was the Joy? Some of the world's greatest composers, like Beethoven, were known to be depressed, even as they created masterpieces. No Joy? Family members may be part of a beautiful vacation, yet not feel great Joy in the experience of it and actually feel relieved when it is over. Communities may come together for an excellent parade, yet not feel Joy during the event.

So how do we get the ultimate . . . Joy, on a consistent basis. When we focus on Joyful producing thoughts, we learn to evaluate events, people and situations as positive, by coming from a place of gratitude, appreciation and fulfillment. Much of this feeling has to do with being thankful to G-d for what he has delivered and the awesome responsibility He has given us. It also has to do with letting go of the past, not worrying about the future, and simply living in the reality of the moment.

FOCUS ON YOURSELF

How do we get to this place of consistent Joy within ourselves? What are some techniques that provide consistent Joy? Peace within can help you consistently find Joy in your life.

Peace Within Yourself

We've found that Peace in one's life starts with Peace within one's self. It is hard, if not impossible, to positively impact Peace within your family and community if you don't have Peace within yourself. In addition, when you do have this inner Peace, we've found that it actually helps to accelerate the Peace within your family and community because you are able to impact them in a positive manner.

It's worth repeating, Peace is tranquility and calm. It is a place of low anxiety and low stress. It is a place where you feel relaxed and your mind, body and heart feel in sync. The following are some tips on how to have Peace within yourself on a consistent basis.

The Fisherman

A businessman was at the pier of a small coastal Mexican village when a small boat with just one fisherman docked. Inside the small boat were several large yellowfin tuna. The businessman complimented the Mexican on the quality of his fish and asked how much time it took to catch them. The Mexican replied, "only a little while". The businessman then asked why he didn't stay out longer and catch more fish? The Mexican said he had enough to support his family's immediate needs. The businessman then asked, "but what do you do with the rest of your time"? The Mexican fisherman said, "I sleep late, fish a little, play with my children, take a siesta with my wife, stroll into the village each evening, and play guitar with my amigos. I have a full and busy life, señor."

The businessman scoffed, "I have an MBA and can help you. You should spend more time fishing and, with the proceeds, buy a bigger boat. With the proceeds from the bigger boat, you could buy several boats. Eventually, you would have a fleet of fishing boats. Instead of selling your catch to a middleman, you would sell directly to the processor and eventually open your own cannery. You would control the product, processing, and distribution. You would need to leave this small coastal fishing village and move to Mexico City, then LA, and eventually New York City where you would run your expanding enterprise."

The Mexican fisherman asked, "But señor, how long will this all take?" To which the businessman replied, "15-20 years." "But what then, señor?" The businessman laughed and said, "That's the best part! When the time is right you would announce an IPO and sell your company stock to the public and become very rich. You would make millions." "Millions, señor? Then what?" The businessman said, "Then you would retire. Move to a small coastal village where you would sleep late, play with your kids, take a siesta with your wife, and stroll to the village in the evenings where you could sip wine and play guitar with your amigos."

The fisherman looked up, waved both hands outward like a game show host displaying a stage full of prizes and said, "You mean, like this?"

Trust in G-d

When we talk about G-d in this book, we are not making reference to any specific religion. Most religions believe there is one Supreme being who watches over them. The G-d we refer to in this book is the G-d of your particular religion.

When you have a full, unfettered trust in G-d, you don't worry about the future. You know that He will give you what you need, teach you what you need to know, and lead you where you are supposed to go. You view challenges as learning lessons from G-d, you perceive people with different points of view as delivering important messages from G-d, and you experience changes in your life as growth opportunities from G-d. You believe that everything happens for a reason and that there are no accidents.

Sometimes our world can feel like Grand Central Station. There is chaos all around us, and we seem to have little control. However, G-d is the one who does have the ultimate control. With His calm and mighty hand, He brings the trains, conductors, and passengers together and somehow sets them to their proper destinations.

To trust in someone means to believe he or she will take good care of you. "In G-d we trust" helps us cultivate optimism about the future. Envision that the Creator, with His glory fills the earth, and His presence is continually with you. Tell yourself, "He is the Master of all that occurs in the world. G-d can do anything He desires. Therefore, it makes no sense for me to put my confidence in anything else but Him, may He bless me."

Rejoice constantly. Ponder with complete faith and trust that the Divine Presence is with you and protecting you. Believe that you are bound up with the Creator, and the Creator is bound up with you. With your every limb and every faculty, fix your focus on the Creator, and the Creator's focus will be fixed upon you!

The Creator can do whatever He wants. If He so desired, He could annihilate all the worlds in a single moment and recreate them all in a single moment too. Within Him are rooted all good and all stern judgments of the world, for the current of His energy runs through each thing. And you say, "As for me, I do not rely upon, nor do I fear, anyone or anything, blessed be He".

Do your best and let G-d do the rest. Live your life right, and trust that G-d will treat you rightly. Treat people well, and trust that G-d will take care of you. "See the G-dliness in all, and you will feel the G-dliness in you." Let go and see obstacles, challenges, and adversities as life lessons, growth opportunities, and developmental moments.

This might sound easier said than done. However, this is where prayer, reading and contemplating religious and other doctrines can give you the knowledge and connection with G-d you need. Spending time with religious figures and in religious settings can help with this too. When you have a deep trust in G-d, you position yourself for the ultimate Peace of mind.

The King and the Servant

A king had a servant who, under all circumstances always said to him: "My king, do not be discouraged because everything G-d does is perfect, and He makes no mistakes." One day, they went hunting and a wild animal attacked the king. The servant managed to kill the animal but couldn't prevent his majesty from losing a finger. Furious and without showing any gratitude, the king said; "If G-d was good, I would not have been attacked and lose one finger". The servant replied: "Despite all these things, I can only tell you that G-d is good and everything He does is perfect; He is never wrong. Outraged by the response, the king ordered that the servant be imprisoned.

Later, the king left for another hunt and was captured by savages who used human beings as sacrifice. On the altar, the savages discovered that the king did not have one finger in place and released him because they considered him to "incomplete" to be offered to their gods.

On returning to his palace, the king authorized the release of his servant and told his servant: "My friend, G-d was really good to me. I was almost killed but for lack of a single finger, I was let go. However, I have a question," the king added. "If G-d is so good, why did He allow me to put you in prison?" The servant wisely replied: "My king, if I had gone with you, I would have been sacrificed because I have no missing finger."

The Big Picture

Life truly is complicated. Have you ever thought about how many cells and organs are in your body? It is mind boggling, and they all need to be working well for you to live a healthy life. How about all the people and events you experience? Probably a significant number every day. Have you ever considered all the things in nature that must work just right for you to get oxygen to breathe, for the sun to grow your food, and for condensation to create your water?

Yes, there is much to our amazing lives. Yet we are not supposed to think about, understand, or worry about all or most of it. In much the same way, when we are experiencing life, we are best served to accept what comes our way as an opportunity to experience a full and rich life, to grow and develop from our challenges, and to accept that we are not always going to understand why this moment is important to the greater purpose of our life.

When we step back from the trees and see the forest of our lives, we can see a beautiful life filled with wonderful miracles every day. We should not allow the zillions of details that make life overwhelm us, paralyze our brain, or cause us unnecessary stress.

Like doing a jigsaw puzzle, stay focused on the big picture on the box cover and trust while applying consistent effort, strategy and patience. When you apply this approach, all the pieces will eventually come together at the right time and in the right way to make something beautiful. However, when we choose to ignore the big picture and look at the puzzle as an overwhelming pile of pieces, shapes, sizes, and colors, we are setting ourselves up for unneeded frustration, stress, and anxiety.

Keep focused on the big picture of life, and remind yourself not to get caught up in all of the small details that you don't understand. Trust that G-d has given you exactly what you need at the time you need it, whether it's a great experience or an important life lesson. When you do this, you will be positioned to minimize your stress and experience more Joy.

Flying on Airplanes

David had avoided flying on airplanes for most of his life because he found himself terrified of crashing. "I couldn't stop thinking about all the disasters I heard about on the news, and every time I thought about flying, I would begin sweating and my heart started pounding. I only felt better by avoiding travel altogether."

But as time went on, David's fear began to prevent him from doing things he wanted to do. He missed his niece's graduation and an important work conference, and his fear prevented him from taking his family on the vacation to the coast. "After years of avoidance, I realized this fear was holding me back, and I had to do something about it."

David met with a therapist, who encouraged him to examine his thoughts about flying and to question their basis in reality. After some research, David had to admit that his fears about plane crashes were greatly exaggerated in his mind—the flight industry is extraordinarily safe, and accidents are rare. The therapist also taught David some relaxation techniques, such as deep breathing and visualization, that he could use any time he felt afraid.

David decided to stop thinking about all the little things that could go wrong, and avoiding his fear. He booked tickets to take his family on their dream vacation. As the flight took off, David focused on the big plane flying him and his family safely to their destination. He kept his breathing calm and even. Whenever thoughts about the possibility of crashing and all the other things that could go wrong with the flight entered his mind, he replaced these thoughts with positive thoughts. He closed his eyes and imagined the plane gliding through the clouds with ease. As the flight progressed, David began to relax. He even enjoyed looking out the window a bit. Anytime he felt himself getting nervous, he gently turned his attention back to his breathing and positive visualization until the feeling passed. When the wheels touched the ground, he felt something more powerful than relief: "I felt so proud that I had faced my biggest fear head-on. As we landed, I felt like this thing that had such a powerful hold on me for so long had finally loosened its grip. I knew that I would probably still feel some anxiety when flying, but now I had the tools to face it with mindfulness. I finally feel free."

You should be aware of what's going on in your mind and take control of your thought-box. Practice staying focused on the big picture and not worrying about all the little things that can go wrong and are unlikely to do so. Get good at. Practice replacing and diverting negative thoughts with positive ones.

Gratitude

Part of the human psyche is naturally resistant to being grateful. Gratitude is a humbling experience, because it demands that we come to terms with the limits of our self-sufficiency. When, however, we acknowledge our dependence on others and express gratefulness, we open up the gates of Joy. We ought to be grateful not only for the gifts we have, but also for the fact that they are provided by someone who cares for us. Realizing that G-d and other people love and care for us is, perhaps, an even greater source of Joy than any other gift.

By not focusing on that which we are missing, we allow our negative feelings to dissipate. When things we appreciate are verbally expressed, they flourish and are amplified. By focusing on and talking about the blessings in our lives, we foster Joyful emotions. If you ritualize gratitude at fixed intervals, you will more likely reap the full Peace benefit. Many religions have a built-in system of rituals that facilitate a steady expression of gratitude for all of the blessings in their lives. Annual holidays are an example, as are weekly gatherings in religious facilities and daily gestures. All of these can help you have consistent Peace within.

Humility

The Rich and Famous, Anschel Rothschild

Everyone has heard of the famous, wealthy banking family, the Rothschilds. The "founding father" of the Rothschild clan, which exists to this day, was Anschel Rothschild, who lived in the middle of the nineteenth century in Austria. He amassed a huge fortune and established a close relationship with the Emperor of Austria, Franz Joseph.

From time to time the Emperor would send visitors to the luxurious and famous palace of Anschel Rothschild. It was the most lavish, luxurious and well-appointed palace in all of Austria, and everyone wanted to see its beauty and glamour.

During one visit Anschel took his guest, an important government official whose position was just under Emperor, on a tour of the palace. He showed him room after room, and the guest was awed by the magnificence of the gold, the silver, the furnishings, the chandeliers, and the imported fabrics. Everything was a sight to behold. There existed nothing like it in all of Austria. When Anschel passed a certain door, he continued walking, but the guest asked to be shown the room behind the door.

"I am sorry," said Anschel. "This is the one room in the palace that I cannot show you." "Why not?" asked the guest. "I would love to see every nook and cranny of your remarkable palace."

"I simply cannot," answered Anschel, and continued walking. The tour concluded, and the official returned to the Emperor, and reported everything he saw. The palace was even more than one could imagine. "However," said the official to the Emperor, "there was one room that Anschel refused to show me." "Why not?" asked the Emperor.

"I do not know. But I can guess. You know how wealthy he is. My theory is that in that room there is a magic moneymaking machine. That is why he is so wealthy. Behind that door must be a machine that creates the wealth of Anschel Rothschild." The Emperor did not know whether to believe his official, so he sent a second government official to see the palace of Anschel Rothschild. The second official came back with the same story, as did a third, and a fourth.

This time the curiosity of Emperor Franz Joseph was greatly aroused, so he decided to go himself and visit the palace. Anschel took the Emperor for the same tour as he did all the other visitors from the Emperor's government. When they reached the "forbidden room," the Emperor asked to go inside and see what was there.

Anschel explained that this was the one place he could not show anyone. After the Emperor insisted, Anschel gave in, and agreed to show the Emperor the secret room. He took out his keys, opened the door, and invited the Emperor to enter.

When the Emperor looked in, he was amazed at what he saw. There, in a small room, was a simple pine box, and some plain white cloth on a table. That was all there was.

"What is this all about?" asked the Emperor. "In my religion, we have strict rules about burial customs," explained Anschel. "When a person dies, he must be buried in a very simple coffin, a plain pine box. And his body must be enveloped in a plain white shroud. This is to maintain the equality of all G-d's creatures. No one is permitted to be buried in a fancy, expensive coffin, or in luxurious clothing. Though some may live affluent lives, and others may suffer dire, abject poverty, in death all are equal." The Emperor responded, "But why is this here in this room?", impressed but still confused.

"At the end of each day, I come to this room, and view the coffin and the shrouds, and I am reminded that even though I have great wealth and power and I have important influence in the highest echelons of the Austrian Empire, I am still one of G-d's simple creatures. At the end of my life, this is the end I will come to like all of G-d's other children. I do this lest after a day filled with high finance and major financial transactions, I think too highly of myself, and develop a bloated sense of myself."

The Emperor was amazed, and in fact, he was speechless. His respect for Anschel Rothschild grew even greater than before. He never questioned the sincerity, honesty, or integrity of Anschel again.

The way we perceive ourselves is crucial to Peace. Both a negative self-image and an inflated sense of self-worth are impediments. When we don't feel good about how we look or what other's think of us, then we cause stress in ourselves. When we think we're better than others or don't treat

37

others well, we will likely be out of sync with the equilibrium of G-d's great world and may feel anxiety as a result.

A greater level of humility occurs when our concept of self slips below the threshold of our awareness, and we are completely focused on fulfilling life's calling. In addition, because we are purposeful beings, we find Joy when we are focused on our purpose.

Humility is the ability to stand in silent awe in the presence of otherness, the presence of G-d, the depth of other people, the majesty of creation, the beauty of the world, the power of great ideas, and the call of great ideals. Humility is the silence of the self in the presence of that which is greater than one's self. Humility allows us to transcend our pettiness, becomes a conduit for the infinite good, and provides a foundation for the Peace within. Humility is not thinking less of yourself, it's thinking of yourself less.

Relationships

Family and friends play an enormous role in our life and well-being. They create a safety net of emotional stability, a foundation to lean on, and a place to grow from. They support us and remind us of what is important, as well as what's not so important. Many people, when asked what brings them Peace and happiness answer, "Spending quality time with family and friends". Family and friends help keep our minds, bodies, and souls at Peace.

The Secret of Sardinia

Psychologist Susan Pinker, in a famous TED talk in 2017, shared the following research she conducted. There is one place in the world where super longevity is common to both genders. This is Sardinia, an Italian island in the Mediterranean between Corsica and Tunisia, where there are six times as many centenarians (people who live over 100) as on the Italian mainland, less than 200 miles away. There are 10 times as many centenarians as there are in North America.

Why? "My curiosity, "said Pinker, "was piqued." She decided to research the science and the habits of the place, and she started with the genetic profile. Pinker discovered soon enough that genes account for just 25 percent of their longevity. The other 75 percent is lifestyle.

So what does it take to live to 100 or beyond? What are they doing right? She visited the place. Wherever Pinker went to interview these centenarians, she found a kitchen party. "Across their life spans, they're always surrounded by extended family, friends, neighbors, the priest, the barkeeper, and the grocer. People are always there or dropping by. They sit, eat, drink, complain, joke, argue, poke fun, sing, party, and spend time together. All of these people are constantly connecting emotionally with many others in their family and community. They are never left to live solitary lives." Dan Buettner followed this up in 2019 with his book Blue Zones. He traveled the world and found other Sardinias. He found that Ikaria in Greece, the Nicoya Peninsula of Costa Rica, and Okinawa in Japan all have approximately ten times more centenarians than the United States and are all utilizing strong social relationships and sense of belonging for longer lives.

The Harvard Study

Psychologist Robert Waldinger is the Director of the Harvard Study of Adult Development, one of the most comprehensive longitudinal studies in history. His findings are fascinating. What keeps us healthy and happy as we go through life? If you were going to invest now in your future best self, where should you put your time and your energy?

As Waldinger puts it, "The Harvard Study of Adult Development may be the longest study of adult life that's ever been done. For 75 years, we've tracked the lives of 724 men year after year, asking about their work, their home lives, their health, and of course asking all along the way without knowing how their life stories were going to turn out. About 60 of our original 724 men are still alive, still participating in the study, most of them in their 90s. And we are now beginning to study the more than 2,000 children of these men. And I'm the fourth director of the study."

Waldinger goes on, "Since 1938, we've tracked the lives of two groups of men. The first group started in the study when they were sophomores at Harvard College. They all finished college during World War II, and then most went off to serve in the war. The second group that we've followed was a group of boys from Boston's poorest neighborhoods, boys who were chosen for the study specifically because they were from some of the most troubled and disadvantaged families in Boston of the 1930s. Most lived in tenements, many without hot and cold running water."

So what did they learn? What were the lessons that came from the tens of thousands of pages of information that they generated on these lives? Waldinger says, "Well, the lessons aren't about wealth or fame or working harder. The clearest message that we get from this 75-year study is this: Good relationships keep us happier and healthier. People who are more socially connected to family, to friends, to community, are happier, they're physically healthier, and they live longer than people who are less well connected. The experience of loneliness turns out to be toxic. People who are more isolated than they want to be from others find that they are less happy, their health declines earlier in midlife, their brain functioning declines sooner, and they live shorter lives than people who are not lonely.

And the sad fact is that at any given time, more than one in five Americans will report that they're lonely."

Waldinger further states "And we know that you can be lonely in a crowd, and you can be lonely in a marriage, so the second big lesson that we learned is that it's not just the number of friends you have, and it's not whether or not you're in a committed relationship, but it's the quality of your close relationships that matters. It turns out that living in the midst of conflict is really bad for our health. High-conflict marriages, for example, without much affection, turn out to be very bad for our health."

When they gathered together everything they knew about the guys in their study at age 50, it wasn't their middle age cholesterol levels that had predicted how they were going to grow old. It was how satisfied they were in their relationships. The people who were the most satisfied in their relationships at age 50 were the healthiest at age 80.

The Harvard study reinforces what the Sardina story revealed. Good relationships can have a major positive impact on one's health. At the same time, with the rise of social media and assisted living in first world countries, isolation and solitude is on the rise and the art of oral communication is on the decline. The long-term impact on our health is concerning. Taking your relationships seriously, both in quality and quantity, can have a significant impact not only in your health but on your Peace within and the Joy in your life.

U.S. Health Resources and Services Administration Study

In 2019, the Health Resources and Services Administration of the U.S. government reported the following:

40% of Americans say they "sometimes or always feel their social relationships are not meaningful"

20% describe themselves as "lonely or socially isolated"

28% of older adults live alone

The report further goes on to state that "loneliness and social isolation can be as damaging to health as smoking 15 cigarettes a day." However, "the good news is that friendships reduce the risk of mortality or developing certain diseases and can speed recovery in those who fall ill."

The type of evidence from these studies shows that strong relationships and caring friendships can positively impact our lives biologically. While relationships can be complicated, they are well worth the investment and can have huge payoffs. When we tap into the love and support of family and friends, we are likely to have and feel more inner Peace and Joy as a result.

Forgiving

Whether it is a family member, friend, or business colleague, holding a grudge and not forgiving them can cause a lot of stress and anxiety in oneself. After all, holding a grudge entails remembering what the person did wrong and having an emotional attachment to that deed. It also requires you to act a certain way toward the person whenever you have contact with them, whether you decide to say something mean, be passive aggressive, or simply hold it in. It may also force you to waste energy and feel anxiety in an effort to avoid the person.

Forgiveness is not a natural instinct. In fact, for most, we want the other person to do something in return or be punished for their act. Often times, we would also like an apology. The problem with this is that we don't control the other person, and often they do not willingly comply with our wants. The question is, "Do we really need to wait for their apology, especially if it costs us some time with our inner Peace?"

If our ultimate want is to have more Peace and Joy in our life, then we need to consider the impact that the actions of others have on our life. When we can put them in perspective and we control what we can, which is ourselves, then we are on the path to more Peace and Joy in our life.

One technique you can use to help yourself forgive more easily is to remind yourself that every person is a special creation of G-d. We are each created in G-d's image and put on this planet for a special reason. Therefore, we should truly love and forgive all of G-d's special creations. In addition, unlike G-d, none of us is perfect. We all make mistakes. Therefore, we should forgive G-d's special creations, our family, friends, and colleagues, when they are simply unable to be perfect like G-d and make mistakes, even when they hurt us. By loving and forgiving all of G-d's creations from deep within our heart, we can more consistently experience Peace and Joy within ourselves.

Another technique is to remind ourselves that each person in our life is living their own life the best way they know how. They may be making some terrible decisions. However, life is complicated, and we all make some bad decisions along the way. Within this mindset, you should also consider that we are all a work in progress. Every day there are opportunities for each of us to grow the knowledge on how to live our best life from our experiences. When you experience that someone hurt you, there is a good chance that they do not know what they are truly doing to you or the impact they are having on you. In fact, if they are hurting you with certain types of actions, they are probably doing the same to others as well. This is why you can leverage an empathetic and caring mentality to forgive them for not understanding what they are truly doing to you and others. You may also be able to use this mindset to sit down with them and have a thoughtful conversation to help them understand what is going on. In this way, by letting go and helping someone else, you will likely experience more Peace within yourself.

Weathering and Growing from Change

Unlike other fruits, which wither and fall off after a single season, the Etrog fruit is a citrus fruit that continues to grow on its tree throughout the entire year, enduring and growing through each season change. The Etrog is the only fruit "that dwells on its tree from year to year." In fact, the Etrog can remain fresh and alive on a tree sometimes up to three, four, or even five years and continue to grow with each season and each year, becoming larger and larger. This sets the Etrog apart from all other fruits, which rot or fall off the tree after their particular season of ripeness has arrived according to its DNA instructions. It is this quality of the Etrog, its ability to weather change and grow from change, which makes it a fruit that can help us understand how to have more Peace and Joy within.

The Etrog 's life, year after year, is analogous to the seasons of human life. The spring bud and bloom of youth, the summer fruitfulness of maturity, the autumn of one's later years, and the wither of life in winter. In addition, a year includes sunny days but also rainy days, exciting days but also monotonous days, success and failure days, blessing and challenge days, straight balls and curve ball days, calm and passionate days, and cold and warm moment days. In short, the year incorporates the full spectrum of human experiences and emotions.

The Etrog's growth through its life, the only fruit which dwells on the tree throughout all the years' seasons and for several years, also teaches us about inner Peace. The art of weathering and growing through all seasons helps us to appreciate the truth that every single experience in life, good and bad, is here to ultimately make life richer and bring out the best in each of us.

Some people can only do well in one particular season. For some, when life is sunny and warm, they thrive. For others, when life is cloudy and cold, they function well. Still, some are at their best when the days are dark and quiet. They are fully alive only in one season. When you take them out of their comfort zone, or when you remove them from their natural habitat, some people wither away or become detached from their tree and roots, from their source of life. When life's circumstances transport them to new and unexpected situations, they often lose their core, vitality, sap, and organic connection with the cosmos, with themselves, and with G-d.

A whole life lived well is one that emulates an Etrog. It is a life that endures the diverse seasons, just like the Etrog, and discovers how to grow bigger and better from each. Every new experience in life, as challenging as it may seem, is an opportunity to discover new horizons, to explore deeper resources, and to find more Peace and Joy within.

The Mind/Body Connection

Dr. John Sarno wrote a book titled *The Mindbody Prescription*. It was written in the 1990s and is believed to have helped many thousands of people achieve Peace and Harmony within. Famous people like Howard Stern and John Stossel brought a lot of credibility to his techniques. Since then, there has been a lot written on its success. There are even many YouTube videos which tell of its miracles. Backs in need of orthopedic surgery are magically repaired and stomach problems quickly healed by using Dr. Sarno's mind-body techniques.

It is interesting when you consider that one of the reasons we exist after our many generations of ancestors' trials and tribulations is that our brains are wired to help us be prepared for what might go wrong. In other words, our brains help us survive. Unfortunately, with so many things that can go wrong in our lives, our brains can be overloaded, and this can impact our inner Peace and Harmony.

Dr. Sarno, an orthopedist, arrived at his approach after noticing that many of his back surgery patients weren't getting the results they expected. He also had a belief that the mind could have a powerful impact on the back. He proved his hypothesis by comparing X-rays of a large number of bad back patients with good back patients. He noticed that more good back patients actually had worse looking back x-rays than bad back patients. Obviously, something was wrong with what he had learned in medical school.

Dr. Sarno then tried a technique that he believed would prove that most bad pain and many other health ailments were caused by the mind. His theory was that the mind was powerful enough to cause significant pain in one's body by cutting off blood to a certain body part. His theory was that the mind did this to distract itself from its problems creating a physical pain to worry about instead.

Next, he came up with a process to prove his theory true. He asked his patients to write a list of all of the things they were worrying about. The list could include being a good mother/father, good wife/husband, good daughter/son, good sister/brother, good friend, as well as concerns about one's job, one's finances, one's commitment to their religion, and so much more.

He then told his patients to tell their brain to "stop causing the pain in my body right now and send blood to my back [or whatever body part is hurting]". Next, he told them to read the list, and for each worry, say "It's ok if I'm not the perfect . . .It's ok if [such and such] happens... I won't let my brain cause pain to my body." They were instructed to repeat this until the pain subsided.

It may sound crazy, but it worked. Many thousands of people have used this technique with amazing successful outcomes.

Scott's Mind-Body Experience

I am one of the people who tried it in 1998 after seeing John Stossel share Howard Stern's and others' stories on the television show 20/20. I was desperate! Feeling terrible back pain, having trouble sitting in meetings, and unable to play tennis. I had been to an orthopedist, a massage therapist, and a chiropractor. I had taken medications and vitamins. Nothing seemed to help. This went on for over a year, and I was certain that I would need the doctor's recommended back surgery. I then saw the special on 20/20 and bought Dr. Sarno's book on the mind-body connection.

The day I read it, I did exactly as I was told. I listed all of the things that worried me. I then told my brain to send blood to my back, that it was ok not to be the best at this and that, and not to worry because everything would be ok. I repeated talking to my brain many times. Within hours of doing this exercise, 75% of my back pain was gone. By continuing the exercise daily, 95% of the pain was gone within a few days. It was a miracle!

With a wife, two young children, a new job, and a new house, it shouldn't come as a surprise that I had been feeling stress. It was also the first time in a while that I had felt significant relief. I was able to remove the baggage from my mind and significantly impact the Peace and Harmony within my mind and body.

This technique is fairly simple, yet it can have a significant impact on your inner Peace. Check it out on YouTube. Many share their stories. Hopefully, this can help you.

Healthy Living

A major component of Peace and Harmony within is a healthy lifestyle. We encourage you to treat your body like a temple. Not only will it help you feel better, but it will also honor G-d. There are four areas of healthy living that we encourage you to consider focusing on: exercise, food, sleep, and mind.

For exercise, there are many ways and approaches. We are not going to recommend a specific exercise regimen. The bigger point is to try and exercise at least 3-4 times per week. Not only will your body feel better, but your mind will also likely be positively impacted. Stretching is also a form of exercise that is often overlooked. It is amazing how complex the human body is and how interconnected the body parts are. For example, back pain could be caused by a problem in your neck or leg. Additionally, our muscles are like rubber bands. If you don't stretch them regularly, they harden and pop over time. Stretch at least 3-4 times per week and you will likely keep your muscles limber and minimize the spreading of pain throughout your body.

For food, again, there are many ways to nourish your body properly. We are not going to recommend a particular diet. The bigger point is to treat your body like a temple and nourish it consistently with good foods in appropriate portions. Natural foods, such as fruits, nuts, and vegetables that are unprocessed will likely make your body feel better than processed foods. After all, this is what our ancestors survived on thousands of years ago and this is what the human body evolved to cherish. Additionally, when in doubt, smaller portions will probably make your body feel better than larger portions.

For sleep, we recommend the current guideline of 6-8 hours of sound rest every night. Naps may also prove to be beneficial. The bigger point is to give your body time to recover every day. If you're having trouble falling asleep, try not to do work, social media, or anything else that will stimulate the mind before you go to bed. Instead, try having a nice conversation with a family member or friend, reading a calm book, listening to soothing music, or doing something else to wind your brain down.

For mind, you can apply the Dr. Sarno techniques discussed in the previous section to connect the mind and body better. You may also want to learn deep breathing techniques to calm the mind. In addition, by getting up a little earlier in the morning and preparing yourself for the day in a quiet place, you may also see a material impact on your mental outlook for the day.

In *Younger Next Year*, Chris Crowley and Henry Lodge include insights into how our bodies were created thousands of years ago, why they evolved the way they did, and how to treat them optimally for our best lives. When you understand your body better, you can achieve more Peace within it.

In Robin Sharma's book *The 5 AM Club*, he discusses getting up an hour earlier than usual and using this time to deep think, journal, exercise, and eat a well-nourished breakfast . . .all by yourself and all in quiet. What a wonderful way to wake up and prepare for a Peaceful, Harmonious and Joyful day!

Conscious Breathing

Breathing is at the core of our existence. From the moment we are born to the time we die, we all must breathe for a healthy life. It is a talent we use immediately when we come from our mother's womb without any formal training, and it is central to the existence of each of us. Fortunately, breathing is something we immediately know how to do when we come from the womb, and we remember how to do without any reminders. Maybe it is from all of the practice we do.

What is interesting about breathing as it relates to Peace within ourselves is that there are actually different ways to breathe. Most people simply breathe regularly into their chest. However, others breathe more deeply into their belly. By consciously and slowly inhaling deeply into your belly and then consciously and slowly exhaling through your mouth, you are likely to feel your body relax and have a sense of calm. If you do this for 5-10 minutes every day, especially with your eyes closed and your mind focused on your breathing, you will likely experience more inner Peace.

Nature

Nature is so beautiful when you take the time to really see it, smell it, feel it, hear it, and be one with it. Take the time to notice the trees with their branches and leaves going in all directions. Feel the blades of grass that individually have a unique texture and collectively form a nice carpet in your yard. Smell the fresh aromas that come from the flowers and trees. Observe the bees that float from flower to flower to make honey. Listen to the crickets chirp and the birds flutter.

Look up at the sky and watch the clouds float by or feel the rain come down and land on your palm. Observe the moon as it changes shape and size night after night. Admire the vast array of colors, shapes, and sizes that surround you from the blooming flowers to the seasonal leaves to the birds looking for food. Try it at sunrise and at sunset.

We all come from nature and will return to nature in the end. We are all part of nature whether we appreciate it or not. When we take the time to simply be with nature, we can be amazed by the way it helps to reduce stress and feel the Peace within.

Expectations

We all have expectations, and these two authors help put them in perspective. Sylvia Plath said, "If you expect nothing from anybody, you're never disappointed." Donald Miller said, "When you stop expecting people to be perfect, you can like them for who they are."

Expectations may be one of the biggest stress creators and negative impactors on inner Peace. For many, they are a consistent source of needless disappointment and anxiety. Expectations on self, on others, and on situations, simply set one up for a negative impact on one's inner Peace. Unrealistic expectations can be even worse and cause emotional pain. This is because life rarely lives up to expectations, and missing expectations often leaves one with negative feelings.

This does not mean that you cannot hope and dream of a great life, a wonderful spouse, an excellent day on the job, and a well running car. What it does mean is that you should not expect every day to go perfectly, you should not expect your spouse to do everything exactly the way you want, you should not expect every day on the job to be without challenges, and you should not expect your car to run without problems from time to time. In fact, when you have the mindset of, "I hope everything goes as planned but I expect there to be some challenges in the day", then you are mentally prepared for whatever comes your way and your inner Peace can then be maintained, even when obstacles and surprises present themselves throughout the day.

In putting expectations in their proper place, you can also remind yourself that only G-d is perfect, so everyone and everything else will not do exactly as planned from time to time. In addition, you can remind yourself that G-d gives us challenges, obstacles, and curve balls to help us grow and develop toward our full potential. In fact, if you want to have an expectation for the day when you get out of bed, then you should expect G-d to give you some growth and development opportunities throughout the day. In keeping this mindset, you are likely to experience more Peace and Joy within.

Time of Rest

True to its name, business is busy-ness. Every day brings a barrage of emails, meetings, decisions, and deals. The same is true for our family life, community organizations and more. Is it any wonder that we lose our center or have anxiety from all of this. What would it feel like to stop and be still and silent for a moment?

We strongly encourage you to take some time every week, every month, and every year to get off of life's merry-go-round and take some time for rest and rejuvenation. Reconnect with family in new ways, try some new activities, and simply do nothing in order to recharge your battery. This may mean doing no business work on the weekend, planning some family vacations throughout the year, or buying a hammock for your backyard and reading on it every week.

In addition, G-d calls for us all to take a day off during the week. "Six days you shall work, and accomplish all your tasks; but the seventh day is a Sabbath unto the Lord Your G-d, in it you shall not do any manner of work, you, nor your son, nor your daughter....for in six days the Lord made heaven and earth, the sea, and all that in them is, and rested on the seventh day. Wherefore the Lord blessed the Sabbath day and made it holy". Exodus 20:08

Sabbath observance has the power to help us with Peace. For 24 hours, we are to view all work we have to do as done and completed. No pushing our lives forward, no need to build, no need to take action, no rushing, no results. Just the freedom to simply be, to be alone, to be with family, to be with G-d, and to enjoy an oasis in the sea of time. Aaron Edelheit's book *Hard Breaks; the Case for the 24/6 Lifestyle* is a great read to help you better understand and implement.

Whatever you do, time of rest can make everything feel better and richer. We hope you will find ways to get away, reconnect, and recharge your batteries for more inner Peace and Joy.

The Act of Completion

Another way to have more Peace in your life is to complete more things. No, we're not asking you to work harder or to do whatever you're doing faster.

If you're like most people, you probably have a To Do list that is very long whether it is written down or in your head. It may consist of things you want to do for yourself, tasks for your spouse, and projects for your boss. These lists can cause a lot of anxiety, and the other problem is that they always seem to exist no matter how hard you work or how focused you are on completing them.

Dianne and Alan Collins describe the Act of Completion on their "QuantumThink" mastery online audio as a way to minimize the anxiety. However, this doesn't mean completing everything on your list. What they do mean is completing what you can and then asking yourself the next best time to complete each unfinished task to give yourself the experience of being complete. By setting a new date for the unfinished tasks, you've actually completed everything for that day and will surely find more inner Peace.

Lighten Up

None of us is perfect, yet it is amazing how hard we can be on ourselves. Often, we are our toughest critics. "What am I doing with my life?", "What is my purpose?", and "How do I make a difference?" are all questions that one may ask oneself. For example, we may be in a meeting and make a comment. Later, we second and third guess ourselves on that comment: "What was I thinking?" The truth in many of these cases is that everyone else in the meeting has already moved on and forgotten about whatever you said. However, we continue to beat ourselves up.

We should remind ourselves that we are not perfect. It is okay to make mistakes, and we should learn from them so we can do better next time. After all, life is about experiences and lessons.

Life is a journey. We are a constant work in progress. Everyday can teach us something. So don't be so hard on yourself. Lighten up! By taking this light and intelligent approach, Peace within is more likely to follow.

.

Inner Peace

If you want to have a Joyful life and help others do the same, you need to find ways to have inner Peace consistently. Whatever you do, it all starts with you. There are many other methods that can help achieve inner Peace that are not mentioned here. They include yoga, Pilates, playing with the family dog, jogging, reading, watching movies, seeing the sun rise, not comparing yourself to other people, life balance, and the list goes on. Whatever you choose to do, we encourage you to find ways to consistently live a calm, stress free, and relaxed life from which Peace and Joy can follow within.

Harmony Within Yourself

Much like Peace, Harmony in our lives starts with Harmony within ourselves. It is hard, if not impossible, to have Harmony in your family and community if you don't have a feeling of Harmony within yourself. Like Peace, we've also found that when you have Harmony within yourself, you can accelerate the presence of Harmony in others.

Harmony within oneself is the feeling when you take your G-d given talents, gifts, passions, and interests and make the most of them. It occurs when your body, mind, and heart work together to get the most out of them. The most Harmonious music in each of us often occurs when we are in the moment and just let it occur almost effortlessly. It also usually happens when we are relaxed, confident, and comfortable being ourselves and doing what we love to do. So much of Harmony within ourselves is about finding our true authentic selves, and then letting it flourish. It also includes not fearing other peoples' opinions of who our best self is.

In addition, when we use our G-d given talents, gifts, passions, and interests to the best of our ability, we are also taking the time to thank G-d for giving them to us and helping to fulfill our purpose. The things we learn and the places we go are not random. They are precisely directed by G-d towards a specific purpose to help us identify and grow our gifts, talents, passions, and interests. We should ask ourselves, "For what purpose did G-d deliver this to me?" We should be keen on finding purpose in everything in our life. We should learn to find growth even from annoying moments. Instead of taking them as stressful experiences, we can choose to interpret them as something helpful to our purpose. When life is about personal pursuits and conquests, it is difficult to identify the purpose of frustrating circumstances. The more mission-oriented we are to find our purpose, the more we are able to convert our hassles into opportunities to discover who we are meant to be and grow toward our most authentic lives and best Harmonic selves.

So how do we get to the place where all parts of our body and life are interwoven together to make a pleasing melody that allows us to be our best selves and experience our most authentic lives? What are some approaches that one can apply? Here are some ways that we believe are helpful.

Each of Us Specially Created by G-d

When you believe in G-d, you know that He took the time to specially craft you. You are not here by accident. You were created for a special purpose and given special talents to help attain that purpose.

We encourage you to identify, develop, and use your special talents to make G-d's world a better place and to fulfill your purpose. You have these special talents, and when you fully trust in G-d, life supports you perfectly to grow and use them. As Golda Meir stated, "You'll never find a better sparring partner than adversity." This is because adversity prepares you for the great life you can live. Adversity, challenges, and obstacles are really lessons and opportunities to develop and grow all G-d has given you.

In addition, you should not be fearful of developing or using your special talents. If they make you happy when using them, you should not worry about what others think. You should simply trust in G-d, know they were given to you specially, and develop them in honor of G-d. As you do this, you should also leverage your Peace within to have your body, mind, and heart relax and calmly bring forth the Harmony created with them. When you do, G-d will smile on you.

Self Remembering

Discover Your Destiny is a book written by Robin Sharma. In this book, he describes how when a baby is born it is fearless and filled with pure love, innocence, infinite wisdom, and boundless potential. A baby is full of life, and beautifully connected to G-d. Young children too are full of energy, curiosity and adventure.

He goes on further to explain that because of outside forces like our parents, teachers, siblings, and friends who have tried to help, we have unconsciously tried to conform with what we believe others think we should be in order to please them. In doing so, we forget about many of our special talents, gifts, passions, and interests that gave us Joyful feelings when we were young. He teaches us to trust the heart when the mind tries to overpower it. Sharma then takes you through a seven-step process to rediscover your special talents and make them yours again. In doing so, he positions you to have your mind, body, and heart sing again like you did when you were young.

In the book, *Designing Your Life: How to Build a Well-Lived, Joyful Life*, Bill Burnett and Dave Evans also share techniques to help you remember your best self. They use word association, ideation, brainstorming, and mind maps to assist you with remembering those times in your life, especially when you were young, when you felt at one with yourself.

Find Your Purpose/Live Your Dreams

In Dianne Collins' book, *Do You QuantumThink? New Thinking That Will Rock Your World*, she discusses the Holomovement of Purpose. She describes this as patterns and clues in our life that are there if we simply pay attention to and discover our special talents and gifts and how they connect to reveal our purpose. These clues and patterns usually reveal themselves at the times that we feel the happiest and best about ourselves. They have been occurring since childhood and have recurred and manifested themselves in different ways throughout one's life. By paying close attention, you begin to realize what your true talents, gifts, passions, and interests are and when you've felt the most Joy. By being aware and in touch with these, they can powerfully help you to have true Harmony in your life consistently.

For example, you may have enjoyed leading your friends in games as a child. As you got older, you found yourself leading school clubs and being team captain of your sports, dance, or cooking team. In college, you may have been an officer in the student council or fraternity/sorority. However, today you may simply find yourself as an employee in a company and a member of social organizations. Consider looking for opportunities in your company to supervise others, offering to be an officer of your social organizations, and thinking of your family as an opportunity to lead the most important people in your life to help live their best lives.

When you become aware of these special talents, gifts, passions, and interests, you may be afraid to take these to the next level or apply them in new areas. However, you are encouraged to listen to your heart. As Paulo Coelho in *The Alchemist* teaches, dream your personal legend and don't fear failure since failing will teach you how to achieve this reality. As Brené Brown teaches in *Daring Greatly*, live your dreams and trust in yourself; as Robin Sharma teaches in *The Monk Who Sold His Ferrari*, live to be all you can be; and as Simon Sinek teaches in *Find Your Why*, live your life with purpose and passion.

Finding your purpose, sharing your gifts and talents with others, and living your dreams are a great way to make the world a better place. They will also help position you for more Harmony and Joy within.

Try New Things

We all have many talents, gifts, passions, and interests within ourselves waiting to be discovered and unlocked. At the same time, it is worth noting how reticent most people are to trying new things. Some people don't want to look or feel foolish. Other people claim they don't have the time. Maybe they think they won't like it.

The reality is that no matter how many things you've tried and have found that you're good at, there is always more potential within you. Not only will you find other things that you're good at and enjoy, every time you try something new and have success with it, you will build your bank of confidence which you can draw on the next time you try something new.

Whether it's cooking, playing a sport, becoming a leader, or singing in a band, you will be amazed by what G-d has given you. We encourage you to take the time and trust in G-d as you try new things.

Talk to Others

When discovering your true talents, gifts, passions, and interests, you may find it helpful to talk to other people. These people can be family, friends, coaches, or teachers who might have noticed something that you may have overlooked. They might see a certain glow in you when you are doing certain things. They may also have ideas of opportunities that may be suitable for you. By talking to them, they may help you discover things about yourself.

You may also want to talk to experts in order to get a better sense of what you need to do to take a talent or a gift to the next level. You may be a good golfer, yet some lessons from a great coach could take you to a whole other level. You may enjoy cooking at home, yet taking some culinary classes could unlock your true chef genius.

Whatever your talents, gifts, passions, and interests are, listening to others can help you experience more Harmony with them.

Be in the Right Question

Dianne Collins in *Do You QuantumThink?* also describes how asking yourself the right questions can sometimes provide amazing answers. She provides techniques and approaches for doing so. By applying this, you can ask yourself the questions that will give you the most insightful and impactful answers about what are your true gifts, talents, passions, and interests.

Questions you may ask yourself are "What do I really enjoy to do?", "What do people come to me for?", "What excites me to get out of bed in the morning?", "When have I been the happiest?", "What was I feeling when I played those drums in high school?", How good did it feel to teach the children's religion class?", and "Why did it feel so good to build that tree house with my son?"

In *The Three Questions*, Don Miguel Ruiz teaches you to nurture yourself by being true to yourself. When you understand how to ask yourself what you need, you can then be all you were meant to be.

So much of understanding yourself better is asking yourself the right questions. By trying different ways to do this, you will likely be pleasantly surprised with the answers you get and the impact they have on your feelings, memories, and interests that you may be overlooking. By being in touch with these special musical notes in your life, you can integrate them into your living for more Harmony.

Nurture Yourself

Just because G-d gave you these special talents, gifts, passions and interests doesn't mean you are making the most of them. This is why you need to nurture them so you can properly and fully play them like an instrument to make musical Harmony within yourself. You may want to take classes, find coaches, or watch videos on the internet to develop them. Whatever talent you're passionate about, we encourage you to develop it.

If it is a newly discovered talent, we encourage you not to worry about what others think as you develop it. Also, ask questions, don't let yourself think it is too hard, and avoid preconceived notions about the challenges ahead. You should remind yourself that children usually learn things faster than adults, so anything you can do to take off your adult glasses and see life like a child may help. Treat this like an adventure, be curious, and apply energy. These could prove impactful in maximizing the Harmony of your instrument within.

In *The Four Agreements*, Don Miguel Ruiz teaches how to be your best self. Being impeccable with your word, not taking things personally, not making assumptions about others, and always doing your best will help you nurture your best self.

In *Grit* by Angela Duckworth, she describes how successful people make the most of their talents and gifts by sticking with them and putting in the extra effort. So many people give up on them before they reach their true potential with them. If you find an interest you enjoy, give it a real chance to develop by putting the necessary time and effort into it. There is a good chance you will be pleasantly surprised by the Harmonious music you are able to create with your special talent.

Inner Harmony

Remind yourself that we've all been given special talents, gifts, passions, and interests. It is our responsibility to discover and develop them. When we do so, we will make more Harmony within ourselves, position ourselves to make more Harmony with others, and likely experience more Joy in our lives.

Joy Within Yourself

Joy is an amazing feeling that we all would like to experience more. In addition, both Deuteronomy 26:11 and Psalms 100:2 state, "Serve G-d with Joy." Therefore, many believe Joy is the soul's ultimate connection with G-d. In sum, we all want Joy and many religions believe we have a moral obligation to live our lives with Joy in all we do.

However, Joy is not automatic, even when you have Peace and Harmony in your life. The following are some tips on how to consistently experience Joy.

See the G-dliness in All

One way to experience Joy consistently is to see the G-dliness in everyone and everything. Whether it is a person, thing, or experience, it was specially created by G-d, and you have been blessed to be a part of it.

Every moment that you are blessed to have your family in your life and are able to share experiences together is a gift from G-d. All the trees, flowers, and birds in nature that surround us outdoors with beauty, smells, and sounds are gifts. All of the opportunities to learn, lead, and, earn money for our family with our jobs are a gift from G-d.

When you look at every moment in your life as specially created for you by G-d, you can thoroughly and appreciatively take it in. All the experiences and challenges are provided to help you grow toward your full potential and live a Joyful life. In fact, when you look at your interactions with every person in your life, including comments they make, as messages from G-d, you will begin more often to feel the Joy within them.

For example, take a can of tuna. A fisherman had to catch the tuna, processing people had to cut it up and package it, and a truck driver had to deliver it from the processing facility to the grocery store you purchased it from. All are gifts from G-d. This example also shows how we are all interconnected with so many more people than we know. In addition, it reveals how we can be positively impacted by so many people we don't even know by simply purchasing a can of tuna at the grocery store.

When you experience these examples and everything else that you are blessed to have in your life as gifts from G-d, you will have more Joy in your life. The Peace and Harmony that you have been cultivating will also help the Joy to be more consistent.

Happiness versus Joy

Joy is often confused with happiness. Yes, Webster's dictionary includes happiness in their definition of Joy, and Joy and happiness can occur at the same time. However, there are many instances when you can be happy with something, yet not feel Joy at the same time.

For example, ice cream may make you happy but probably does not consistently bring you Joy when you eat it. You may be happy with the car you own, but you don't feel Joy every time you drive it. You may be happy with your job, but you don't feel Joy every time you walk into your office.

At the same time, you are more likely to experience Joy when you are happy. This is because happiness positions you for Joy. Happiness usually comes from outside stimuli, while Joy is a feeling from inside. If you're not happy with whatever you're doing, it will be difficult to feel Joy. Accordingly, happy people experience more Joy in their lives.

So how can you have more happiness in your life so that you are positioned for more Joy? Happiness often comes from a place of gratitude and appreciation. Being thankful for your family, friends, health, job, talent, and gifts can be a great way to experience consistent happiness. Sometimes finding happiness may simply mean taking the time to truly be in the moment and experience rather than letting your mind drift or multi-task. Again, you're more likely to experience Joy when you're happy, so we encourage you to find your happy place.

One of the secrets to Joy is to stop focusing so much on "how happy I feel", and instead utilize our life to produce benefits for others. If you wallow all day in yourself, trying to figure out why you feel this way or that way, you often will remain stuck in an elusive search for Joy. It is the very pursuit of Joy that often thwarts it. Joy is a product of a life well lived, when you are doing what you're supposed to do and when you are true to yourself and your mission in this world.

The Highway Story

Once upon a time, a king had a great highway built for the people who lived in his kingdom. After it was completed, but before it was opened to the public, the king decided to have a contest. He invited as many of his subjects as desired to participate. The challenge was to see who could travel the length of the highway the best, and the winner was to receive a box of gold.

On the day of the contest, all of the people came. Some of them had fine chariots. Some had fine clothing and fancy food to make the trip a luxurious journey. Some wore their sturdiest shoes and ran along the highway on their feet to show their skill. All day long, they traveled the highway. Each one, when he arrived at the end, complained to the king about a large pile of rocks and debris that had been left almost blocking the road at one point and that had gotten in their way and hindered their travel.

At the end of the day, a lone traveler crossed the finish line warily and walked over to the king. He was tired and dirty, but he addressed the king with great respect and handed him a small chest of gold. He said, "I stopped along the way to clear a pile of rocks and debris that was blocking the road. This chest of gold was under all of it. Please have it returned to its rightful owner." The king replied, "You are the rightful owner." "Oh no," said the traveler, "This is not mine. I've never known such money." "Oh yes," said the king, "you've earned this gold, for you won my contest... He who travels the road best is he who makes the road better for those who will follow."

This is true of the voyage of life. The deepest Joy emerges when you stop focusing on yourself and your emotions and you instead bring light to the world around you. Instead of searching your whole life for what you need, search for what you are needed for. Find a mission and a purpose which transcends you and devote yourself to it. Ask yourself these questions. Do I have a real purpose in my life, purpose created by something which transcends me and my ego? Am I dedicated to a meaningful cause beyond my own self-gratification and comfort? Search and find answers to the questions, and more Peace, Harmony, Joy are likely to follow. Good luck. Find your treasure chest of gold!

Circumstances Do Not Have to Control Joy

The Soviet Prison

In surviving Stalin's Gulag prison in Siberia, Reb Mendel explained that one of the keys to survival for the prisoners was not allowing their surroundings and situation to dampen their spirits. They made carnivals, and many played with cards and tried to be upbeat.

One time, while they were passing their free time and telling jokes, all of a sudden one of the prisoners in the barracks began sobbing and couldn't stop. After a few minutes, the leader of the group said to him, "Tell me, why are you crying now? We can't let them realize that we are broken!"

The man replied, "How can I not cry? We are trying to have an enjoyable time, and this reminds me of where I was a mere six months ago. Then I truly had an enjoyable time. I was the chief physician in the city. Every difficult medical issue was brought to my attention. Everyone tried to make sure that I, and not one of the numerous doctors under me, treat them and their family. I was invited to every important function. I was truly happy.

Now look at me. No one cares or knows that I am a famous physician. All the years of studying and experience was for nothing. Indeed, I feel as if I am nothing, so how can I not be sad? The leader of that group stood up and stated, "Why do you think your situation is so unique. I was the top lawyer in the entire region. I was able to demand a premium price for my services, and I too was invited to every important meeting, and now, I am in the same mess you are in."

Another prisoner then stood up and said, "Your woes are nothing compared to mine. I used to be the most feared person in the entire region. Everyone trembled when they saw me. I sent countless innocent people to prison and even to death, just to put a fear in everyone. And then one day my subordinates gleefully arrested me on trumped up charges, and I was reduced to a nothing."

This conversation was continued by each person, saying how he was reduced from his importance into a nobody. The entire time Reb Mendel listened with amusement. A smile was noticed on his face by a few of his fellow prisoners, and they pointedly asked him why he thought this was amusing. "Didn't you lose some prestige or importance?" they inquired. "What were you before you were sent here and what are you now?"

Reb Mendel replied, "Before I was arrested, I tried to be a good person and serve the Creator to the best of my ability. That same mission remains with me until this very day. The place and surroundings may be different, but the goal remains the same."

As Viktor Frankl stated in his book, *Man's Search for Meaning,* about his time in a concentration camp during World War II, "circumstances do not determine Joy, it can be found anywhere and anytime." In fact, he was able to find Joy in the smallest of places, and he used this as one way to survive.

Studies have also found that low-income people experience as much or even more Joy than higher income people. This fact is believed to stem from the additional anxiety that comes from the more complex lifestyle and spending decisions in the lives of people with more money.

Appreciate what you have, not what you don't. Keep your connection with G-d strong. In doing so, your circumstance will always be good, and you will be positioned for consistent Joy within.

Observer-Created Reality

An essential factor of experiencing Joy is our attitude towards life, towards yourself, towards other people, and towards events and situations. Your attitude towards any event or situation is not based on its objective reality but on your own subjective evaluation of that event or situation.

As Dianne Collins teaches in *Do You QuantumThink?*, we all live in an Observer-created Reality. It is the reason that you and someone else can hear the same speech or go to the same movie and have completely different experiences of each. We all bring our individual life experiences and thoughts to every situation and then use these to interpret our reality of them.

While you can't change your life experiences, you can change your interpretations of them. You can choose to observe your life appreciative of what you have or you can choose to dwell on what you don't.

For example, if you lost your job, you could interpret this as a terrible, unfair life event. On the other hand, you could choose to observe this as a message from G-d that there is a better way for me to earn a living. You could also choose to observe this as a message from G-d that consistently delivering your projects late is not good and as an important lesson to take to that next job. Following this line of logic through, you may even be able to feel Joy in the experience of losing your job as you are blessed to learn these life lessons.

Another example of an Observer-created Reality is that we all have jobs whether it's in the business world, at home, at school, or at some other place. We can each choose to have a reality that our job is drudgery or that I would rather be doing something else. However, we can also each look at our job as honoring G-d in that each of us is contributing to G-d's wonderful world. If we choose the latter, it will help us feel more alive in all our jobs as we live with Joy.

Being versus Doing

Another tip for experiencing Joy is being in the moment with whatever you are involved in as opposed to simply doing it. This can be at home, at work, or at an extracurricular activity.

For example, parents may just feel like they are doing their job when they read a bedtime story to their child night after night. However, if they can be in the moment each time with the child, they can have a Joyful experience. For example, they can feel Joy in the moment by recognizing they have this precious gift cuddled up to them. They can feel Joy in having this beautiful child hang onto every word out of their mouths. They can feel Joy in knowing their child will sleep like an angel because of the story and experience just shared.

In another example, you can be at work answering customer complaints by phone, doing your job, and counting down the minutes until your next break or until the workday is over. On the other hand, you can be in the moment as you know that you are helping another person with a problem, making their life better, and using some of your G-d-given talents. In doing this, you can turn your day on the job into a Joyful experience.

Another trick to being in the moment is to keep the mind focused on the task at hand or the experience you're in. In our busy world, we often try to multi-task. Unfortunately, this almost guarantees that whatever you're doing, neither the tasks nor the experiences will be Joyful simply because your mind is not deeply connected or focused on either of them. Spencer Johnson's book *The Present* is a great read for helping to teach you to live in the moment.

In *Do You QuantumThink?*, Dianne Collins teaches of Being in One Conversation. This technique can be helpful when you're talking to someone and want to have a Joyful experience. If you're simply listening to their words and waiting for an opportunity to say something in response, this is actually being in two conversations: yours and theirs. If you're truly listening to what they're saying and let the words and conversation flow naturally, then you're more likely to experience Joy in this interaction.

Dianne's Observer-created Reality technique described earlier can also help you be in the moment. By simply being grateful for the opportunity to utilize your gifts and talents for G-d, whether it is at home, at the office, or anywhere else, you create the opportunity to be in the moment and a Joyful experience.

Good Thoughts

The emotional consequences of events are largely up to us. Our thoughts control our emotions, and our emotions often control our actions. This is why our minds have a lot of impact on the life we experience. It is interesting to note that the letters forming the Hebrew word "B'sameach" meaning "Joy" are similar to the letters that spell "Machashavah", meaning "thought".

As amazing as it may sound, you can choose your thoughts. Focus on Joyful, productive thoughts instead of negative thoughts. Evaluate events, people, and situations as positively as possible, such as giving people the benefit of the doubt. When things are going well, take a moment to savor and appreciate what has just occurred. Let the good thoughts flow.

We actually have the ability to keep good thoughts in our mind and push bad thoughts out. Now this may sound hard to some people. However, if you practice, you can really do it.

For example, think of a moment that brought you great Joy. It could be the birth of a child, a family get together, winning an award, a beautiful hike in the woods, or watching the sunset. Whatever it is, try to remind yourself of it whenever you let your mind drift to bad thoughts. You will likely be pleasantly surprised about how your mind changes.

Having gratitude and appreciation can also help you have good thoughts. Instead of looking at a situation and saying "Why me?" you can look at it and say "Thank You G-d" for teaching me a good lesson. For example, if your boss just finished telling you he was disappointed in your work, you could feel sad and have bad thoughts like "I hate my boss", I'm going to quit my job", or "I can never please him". On the other hand, you could take a deep breath and ask yourself "Could I have done better, and if so, how?", "Maybe this is a reminder that I should start looking for that new job so I can maximize my talents", or "Maybe I should take that inter-personal skills class I've been thinking about so I can better connect with people."

Having good thoughts about yourself, family, and community will help you position yourself for more Joy in your life. In addition, when you use these good thoughts to help bring Peace and Harmony into your life, more Joy is likely to follow.

Flow for Joy

In Mihaly Csikszentmihalyi's book *Flow*, he describes the psychology of optimal experience as a pathway to Joy. Though he doesn't specifically discuss Peace and Harmony as pathways to Joy, what he does present are athletes, musicians, chess masters, and more that have a deep sense of enjoyment when they are able to concentrate on their talents.

People with some of the most amazing accomplishments and experiences of Joy were so focused on their task at hand, had such confidence in what they were doing, and felt such a free-flowing sense of movement that they were able to attain this optimal experience. In some of the most challenging situations, they described feelings of almost effortless unconsciousness as they experienced these unique levels of Joy.

We believe this can be applied to anything you do when you tap into your Peace and Harmony and allow things to flow. It can be routine activities at home or at the office, or it can be a major sports competition. Simply allow your Peace and Harmony to flow to new levels of Joy.

While G-d gifted each of us with many talents and gifts, deeply appreciating them allows them to flow fully. The Peace presents the time and place and the Harmony presents the instruments to be played fully and brilliantly as you connect deeply with G-d in Joy.

The Five Senses

One way to experience Joy is to be in touch with your five senses. These are taste, smell, sight, sound, and touch. We use them all the time and usually take them for granted. However, with a little practice, you will be amazed how much Joy they can create. The old saying "Stop and smell the roses" applies here and can be a great way to create Joy in your life, both literally and metaphorically.

For example, you may like vanilla ice cream. After dinner, you get a bowl of it and eat it. Yes, it may have tasted good. It may also have made you happy. However, did it bring you Joy? Perhaps if you took the time to taste the vanilla flavor, feel the cool, creamy texture on your tongue, smell the scent of the vanilla beans used to create it, and even observe the perfect two scoops placed in your bowl by your spouse, you may experience Joy in this dessert.

In another example, you may go jogging on a path near your house to get some exercise so you can eat ice cream for dessert that evening. Will this be a Joyful experience? Perhaps if you observed all of the beautiful flowers and trees around you, listened to the songs of the birds chirping, and smelled the great aroma from nature, you might experience Joy in working up a sweat and burning some calories.

Our five senses are particularly interesting when you consider that all of us don't have the same level of sensitivity for each one. Blind people can't see and deaf people can't hear. What's even more interesting is that the sensitivity in the other senses of these people is usually heightened. For example, blind people often have a heightened sound and touch sensitivity, and deaf people usually have extra sight perception.

G-d gave all of us senses, it is up to each of us to take the time to appreciate them. When you bring them into your awareness, you will likely be pleasantly surprised by the Joy they unlock within you.

The Gift of Giving

Another way to consistently feel Joy is to share your talents and gifts with others. By taking the time to teach what you know, you can help to change another person's life. This is your opportunity to give back in honor of G-d, and it is usually an amazing feeling, especially when your student shows true progress.

There are also people who don't have the confidence or ability to do something and the act of inspiring, helping, supporting, caring, and encouraging these people to grow can be extremely Joyful. An added bonus to teaching is that it often challenges you to understand your craft more deeply. By understanding your talent better, you may experience additional Joy, especially if you take them to a whole other level.

Most religions encourage giving of money or other material items to honor G-d. Giving of your time and money to charities is another way to have this good feeling. Giving consistently from the heart without expecting anything in return is a freeing feeling.

Sharing your G-d given talents, your time, your money, whatever it is, simply because you have the opportunity should make you feel good inside. Feeling good inside can only help you feel more Joy.

Inner Joy

As you strive to experience more Joy within, observe children, as they seem to effortlessly and purely be in the moment and filled with Joy many times throughout their day. You were a child once upon a time, and you still have the opportunity to tap into this.

Remind yourself that life is a journey and none of us is perfect. When you find yourself not feeling as much Peace, Harmony, and Joy as you would like, remind yourself that there is always tomorrow to change and to work on these techniques to feel them more often. Don't let the goal of less stress and more Joy cause you more stress in your life.

When we find true Peace within our mind and body, are true to ourselves, and allow our true gifts and passions to play together in Harmony, then we are more likely to experience consistent Joy. By using the techniques we've just described, you will more likely be able to feel Peace, Harmony, and Joy within and to have a special connection with G-d more consistently.

FOCUS ON YOUR FAMILY

Joy with others starts with Joy within ourselves. Now that we've worked hard on ourselves, we can utilize these lessons and great feelings with the others who are most important to us: our family.

We define "family" as any group of people that you have close relations with. Obviously, this includes your real-life family: a spouse, mother, father, brothers, sisters, grandparents. However, it also includes your work family: boss, peers, subordinates, your spiritual community, your athletic teams, and your performing arts groups. These people are ones that you form close relationships with and are often the source of love and support, as well stress and anxiety, in your life.

Your family is a blessing. G-d has given you these people to learn from, to get you through tough times with, and to help you have a full and loving life. They are also some of your best sources of Joyful experiences. However, for many, Joy within their family is easier said than done. We will now provide our approach to more consistent Peace, Harmony, and ultimately Joy with the ones you care most about.

Peace With Family

Your family is a special gift. When we have Peace with family, we have happy, healthy relationships with these important people. The members genuinely respect each other, are thoughtful with their words and actions, and do not intentionally cause harm to each other. Now, we will share some tips on how to have Peace with your family.

See the G-dliness in Them

When you deeply believe in G-d, you understand that everyone is a special creation of G-d. Every person is put on the earth for a special reason, just like you. When you take the time to get to know and appreciate the specialness in every person in your life, especially your family members, it makes a big difference in how you feel about them. When something potentially goes wrong with the relationship, you now are positioned to seek to right it because of their importance to you and your understanding of who they are. There is no need to hold grudges.

We also want to consistently keep in mind that all of the people close to us are living daily challenges that G-d has provided for their growth. They may do things sometimes that seem hurtful to you but are simply responses to their own challenges. As humans we also develop habits of how we treat others, and people in our lives may not treat others well simply because they are unaware of their own bad habits. When they say or do something that may be hurtful, you can more easily forgive them since you know that they're not perfect . . . only G-d is. They may simply be having a rough day or expressing a bad habit.

By seeing the specialness in your family members yet remembering that they're not perfect, unlike G-d, you should be positioned to have more Peaceful experiences with them. When they do or say something that you don't like, simply remind yourself of their G-dliness and allow yourself to keep the Peace with them.

Create an Intent

One of the biggest challenges we have in relationships with those close to us is that we take each other for granted. The excitement that one may have felt early on in a marriage or in joining a team may now be gone. We may have worries about the relationship. Also, when one of your close relations does or says something that could be taken the wrong way, you may immediately take it in a bad way without giving it much thought. It is easy to fall into this trap and lose the Peace with family members.

One approach to helping with this is to use an approach created by Dianne Collins and taught by her husband and business partner, Alan Collins, who is a Master QuantumThink Coach. This approach is called "Creating an Intent". An Intent in this case is a deep feeling and awareness in your mind, your heart, and your soul for the Harmony of the relationship. You treat it like it exists, even when the relationship does not go perfectly. You understand that relationship issues are relationship strengthening opportunities, as you focus on and stay aware of the Harmony in the relationship.

An Intent may be that you "want to have a great experience of a person in your life". Another Intent may be that you "want a person in your life to have a great experience of you". When you set these Intents and genuinely try to set your mind up for them prior to interactions with these people, there is a good chance that you will be pleasantly surprised. By simply focusing on having a great experience with someone, the relationship can actually shift in that direction.

Peaceful relationships are often results of Intentional behavior. Create Intents for loving, caring and understanding relationships and experience the results of reduced stress, increased calm, and more Peaceful family relations.

Listen from Not-Knowing

Another challenge we have with family members is getting in a rut and feeling like there is something wrong with the relationship. We also take them for granted and do not give them the attention they deserve, especially in daily conversations.

For example, when a husband has a conversation with his wife after a long day at the office, he may feel like she is essentially saying the same thing every night. She might say, "I took the kids to school, bought groceries, cleaned the house, and made dinner." He might say, "Sounds like you did a lot. My day was busy with customers and meetings". They can both come away from the conversation feeling like the other does and says the same thing day after day. This can lead to feelings of boredom and being unloved, and it can add stress to the relationship.

One approach to helping with this is to use another Dianne Collins approach called "Listen from Not-Knowing". The technique to use here is to act like you've just met and never had a conversation with this person, and then to listen deeply to what they have to say. Words that used to mean nothing to you or seemed redundant may now take on a new meaning, and your conversation will likely go in new and different places, thus strengthening the relationship.

For example, if the wife says, "I took the kids to school", then the husband could say, "Did you talk to anyone there?" or "Did you observe our child doing anything with their friends?" This will likely lead to the wife sharing more about her experience. These additional conversation points should lead to a deeper connection and a more satisfying and Peaceful relationship.

Take a Deep Breath

When you're in a disagreement with a family member and you begin to feel your emotions creep in, this may be a signal to you that it is time to take a deep breath. This is especially important if you want to keep the Peace in the moment and for days, weeks, months and even years to come. This is because if you don't, you might say something you later regret. As Solomon once said, "The tongue has the power of life and death."

When we say take a deep breath, this can mean literally breathing in slowly and deeply so that you can calm yourself and think clearly. This can also mean stopping the conversation and asking the other person or people if you can come back to it at a later time when you have had more time to think about it. This extra time will give your emotions the opportunity to subside. You may even want to use the breathing technique described in the Peace Within Yourself section to help get you grounded and then think through the best way to come back to the conversation.

Take the time to think before responding to a stressful situation and give yourself time to decompress from an emotionally charged conversation. This can make a big difference in maintaining a Peaceful relationship.

The Power of Forgiveness

Mahatma Gandhi said, "The weak can never forgive. Forgiveness is an attribute of the strong". In other words, it is easy to hold a grudge and not let another person redeem themselves to you. After all, you simply maintain the emotions and memories attached to the act that hurt you. However, to get past these, it takes effort and will to forgive them. If you want to have Peaceful relationships with others, especially your family, you should consider working to strengthen your skills at this.

The challenge with so many of these situations is that the act that the other did felt hurtful and seemed wrong to you. This all may be true. However, the question is whether you can get past it to have Peace with the person and more Joy in the relationship. There are a number of techniques you can use.

You can try to see the G-dliness in them to forgive them. In using this technique, we view them as a messenger from G-d, even if they hurt your feelings. When you apply this technique, whatever they did or said was simply a message from G-d to help you be a better person, learn a lesson, or be aware of something you may not have noticed.

The Building Campaign

We both had this experience when Yossi brought his congregation leadership together to discuss its future. For about half of the leaders, their number one issue was that they were disappointed that a building had not been built for a number of years on the land they had purchased. When we met after the meeting to discuss this, Yossi explained that he felt hurt and saddened. "How could they say such a thing? Don't they know how hard we work? Don't they see how much progress we have made?"

Scott encouraged Yossi to use this technique. "These people are messengers from G-d. Perhaps they are simply reminding us that it is now time to build".

Shortly thereafter we launched the Building Campaign to build an enrichment center on the land and the rest is history. In addition, Yossi was able to see the G-dliness in each of the leaders and not only forgive, but "Thank" them. Not only did Peace happen but it also positioned Harmony and Joy to follow in a significant manner.

Other techniques that we've already shared that can help you forgive are "Observer Created Reality" and "only G-d is perfect". By using these, you can experience previously upsetting conversations in a positive manner with your family members.

For example, if you had a meal with your family member and they said "You shouldn't eat that. It will make you fat. I'm concerned about your weight." Many people would be hurt by such a comment. Afterall, no one should tell you what you should eat, and no one should insult you for the way you look. However, when you utilize these Intent techniques, then you can look at these comments differently. Perhaps this is a lesson from G-d to educate you on a health issue. In addition, maybe they don't understand that the comments hurt your feelings. If you perceive the conversation from these perspectives, perhaps you can also use it as an opportunity to sit down with the family member and explain in a nice, loving, and caring way that the comments hurt, even though you know they were simply trying to help. Now that they are aware that they hurt you, you can "Thank" them for their concern and ask them not to make comments like that in the future. In doing this, you have forgiven them, and you have set up the family relationship for more Peace and Joy going forward.

Yes, it is nice when the other person apologizes first. It is often even better when they make restitution to you by telling you that you were right, changing a previously made decision, or giving you a gift. However, when you take these acts of apology as requirements for forgiveness out of the equation, you help the relationship because you begin the process of healing and accelerate toward the Peace, Harmony, and Joy.

It Takes Two to Tango

Do you realize that you can live a life where you never have another fight with a family member again? Yes, it is true. You have the ability to have Peace with everyone in your family on a consistent basis.

After all, a fight with a family member occurs only when both say or do things to hurt the other. If one family member does something to hurt the other, and the other doesn't do something to hurt the other in return, then what you have is one or both family members with hurt feelings . . . but not a fight.

You may be saying to yourself, "Am I simply supposed to let them hurt me?", or "How am I supposed to maintain any self-respect?", or "What if I'm right and they're wrong?". The list could go on endlessly. After all, if someone hurts you, why should you simply take it?

The key point here is that this is not about taking it or sucking it up. It is about learning to choose your responses to those who are important in your life when they intentionally or unintentionally hurt you. Your mind is powerful, and you have the opportunity to use it for the greater good of attaining Peace and Joy with your family member.

So how do you go about this and retain dignity at the same time? Well, there are actually many ways. One way is to keep good thoughts and Intent in your mind such as "I want to have a Peaceful, Harmonious, Joyful relationship with this person", "I believe that they want to have good relationship with me", "I know that they're human, not perfect, and I can accept their mistakes", and "I know there is a calm way to respond to their comments either now or at a later time from a place of caring and careful thought".

For example, if your spouse yells at you for not doing as they asked, you could later apologize for not listening, tell them you will try to do better next time, and ask them not to yell at you if you do it again. You may also want to try to do a better job listening next time. However, in marriage this can be a common theme. If so, you may want to calmly respond that "this keeps coming up, and I love you, so how about we meet with a marriage therapist who can help us to better understand each other". There are many ways this can play out. The key point is keeping the Peace to position yourself for a more Harmonious and Joyful relationship.

In another example, your teenager may have come home after their curfew. When you told them they were grounded per the family rules, they screamed at you and said some mean things. Again, you could say some things back that could escalate the situation and become a fight. On the other hand, you could also choose to wait until the next day when things will be much calmer and emotions will have subsided. You could then sit down with them and remind them that the reasons for the curfew are to help them be safe and to keep you from worrying about them. You may still follow through with their punishment, though they may or may not agree with it. However, you have kept the Peace and hopefully positioned yourself for more Harmony and Joy with them.

Yes, life with family members can be complicated. So many times we simply react to comments without even thinking. These reactions are simply habits, and when we retaliate, they impact the Peace between you and your family member. Like any habit, you simply need to be aware and committed to breaking the habit. Many habits take 60-90 days to form or break. Be committed to no longer feeding the fire or doing the tango fight. Breaking this habit can pay huge dividends in your future Peaceful, Harmonious, and Joyful relationship with your family members.

Empathy and Compassion

We should remind ourselves that the people who are most important in our lives are facing many challenges every day whether it is with their health, with other family members, at their job, in their social life, or more. Being human means our life isn't perfect. In addition, G-d gives us challenges to help us grow and develop toward our full potential.

Because we know our family members are all dealing with challenges every day, sometimes they will become frustrated, sad, or even upset. These feelings may come across as meanness to us. We can then choose to respond back with meanness, or we can choose to maintain the Peace by responding with empathy and compassion from a place of love and care in our heart.

After all, we know they are good people. They are simply just not perfect in the way they always handle their challenges. Simply take the time to remind yourself that life is not always easy for our family members, and we can respond with love, support, and care in every interaction we have with them. In doing so, we can have a Peaceful, Harmonious, and Joyful relationship with each of them.

Family Peace

Your family is a special gift. All the people who you hold close can play an important role in your Joyful life. Try committing yourself to not fighting with them. This doesn't mean you have to feel like they always get their way or that you're being disrespected. Simply try to find ways to keep the Peace. When you do this, you will better control your emotions, have more thoughtful conversations, and find more common ground. As a result, you will experience more happy and healthy relationships and are positioned for more Harmony and Joy with these important people in your life.

Harmony With Family

Again, our families are our real-life families plus others that you have a close relationships with. The goal is to have Harmony with them where everyone is free to be their best selves, appreciated for what they bring to the group, and is a part of making beautiful life music together. Here are some tips we've found for having and creating more Harmony within our families.

G-d Created Each of Them Specially

Your family did not come together by accident. G-d created each member specially and brought everyone together carefully to make Harmonious music and Joy together.

One of the most interesting phenomena with families is how everyone is different, unique, and special. For children birthed from the same parents, raised in the same home, and with many of the same shared experiences, it is amazing how different each turns out to be. You then mix in a husband and wife from different families, in-laws, aunts, uncles, and more. This uniqueness and specialness is also seen on sports teams and business teams, where teammates come from different communities, ethnic backgrounds, colleges, and more.

At the same time, it is because of these different, unique, and special characteristics that G-d has created in each family member that beautiful Harmonious music can be made. Can you imagine what an orchestra would sound like if everyone played the same instrument? A basketball team wouldn't stand a chance of being great if everyone was a great shooter, but no one could pass or rebound. A business would not succeed if everyone was excellent at designing and engineering, but no one was good at selling.

The great leaders, coaches, and conductors know how to take the G-d created specialness in each member of their team and get them to make Harmonious music together. They are able to appreciate the unique skills, gifts, personalities, and so much more in their team members and blend them together into a beautiful team. In addition, the greatest teams often have the players lead and conduct themselves to create even more Harmonious music.

In much the same way, G-d has created our families with individuals that have unique perspectives, experiences, talents, and gifts. Each of us has an opportunity to be a leader, coach, or conductor and to have a family that makes beautiful music together. When you have Peace, Harmony, and Joy within, you can now share it with your family to have the same with them.

Trust is the Foundation

Trust within a family is so important. If you don't know whether another family member is being truthful or dishonest, it is very hard to let your guard down and be your best self with them.

In order for the music of life to emerge between two or more people, there must be a true trust. This is more than saying "I trust you" or signing a document that "we will trust each other". True trust is about knowing in your heart and soul that you can be yourself and not worry about being mistreated by the other for being yourself. It also means that you are not worried about the others giving their best and that you know everyone is acting with their best of intentions for all involved. With true trust in place, you and the others are able to focus on being your best and maintaining your Harmonic, relaxed, and confident states of mind.

Interestingly, children are born with trust. They trust fully in their parents and family to take care of their needs. Somewhere along the way their life unfolds, they have experiences, and that trust erodes. However, your family should be the people you trust the most. They should be there for you for the ups and downs and the thicks and thins. This is why it is so important you work on trust in order to have Harmony and Joy with your family.

Two key elements of trust are character and competence. It is hard to trust someone if they don't have both. Character is about doing the right thing regardless of the situation. You can trust someone to have your back.

However, if they're consistently cancelling outings or talking behind your back, you might question their character. Competence is about doing things the way you believe they should be done. If someone consistently leaves clothes on the floor or forgets to pick up the dry cleaning, trust is impacted. This also applies to your colleagues at work where an employee who is consistently late on projects may have their character questioned, and a peer who doesn't seem to do good work may have their competence questioned. In both cases, it will be hard to trust them on projects going forward.

The bottom line: trust is fundamental to good relationships. Yes, you may be able to keep the Peace with your family members. However, if you don't have trust, there is unlikely to be Harmonious music and Joy created.

Take Time Get to Know Family Members

When you take the time to really know another person, you see them for more than is on the surface. They are more than a sibling, a parent, a child, a co-worker, or a teammate. At work, people are more than a job title and level. Everyone comes from somewhere, everyone has story, everyone has interests, everyone has skills, and everyone has challenges. By taking the time to understand and share these, you are now on track to have a more Harmonious relationship.

Taking time to get to know another person may include taking them out to lunch, stopping by their office for a chat, or playing a game of cards. Simply finding opportunities to change up the structured environment is another way to Listen from Not-Knowing. A person who you think you know a certain way is now different due to the unique experience, which likely will lead to you getting to know them better and appreciating them more.

For example, by taking your sister out for lunch and learning that she is struggling with her job and boss, you may be more empathetic when she comes late to dinner after work. It could be a colleague who tells you about their mother with cancer which might lead to you better understand them when they are late on a project. It could also be a sports team member who shares the challenges they're having at home, such as their spouse not wanting them to play on the team, which may lead to you better understanding why and being empathetic when they miss some practices.

In Gary Chapman's *5 Love Languages* book, he teaches about how getting to know the important people in your life can help you understand how to speak their love language when it comes to strengthening relationships. Additionally, in *Men Are From Mars, Women are From Venus*, John Gray teaches how to better understand and develop relationships with the opposite sex. When you better understand your family members, you can be empathetic and concentrate more on making beautiful Harmonious music when you're together.

Communication is Key

Communicating appreciation and kindness to others is a great way to build Harmonious relationships. As Mark Twain said, "I can live for two months on a good compliment." However, there are often times when compliments are not what one wishes to communicate. Instead, there is a problem that may need to be addressed. This is where proper communication becomes so important. Depending on the person and the situation, you should be thoughtful with what you say.

Take the time to consider the best way and time to communicate. Often when needing to address an important problem, a face-to-face conversation is better than a phone call, which is often better than an email. Also not trying to fix the problem in the heat of a disagreement or when someone is rushed can help the communication have a better impact. In addition, looking for a win for everyone involved in the communication can be helpful. You should remind yourself that if your overall goal is Joy within your family, then being right all the time may need to take a backseat. Instead, try to find the win for each family member, including you, that allows all to maintain their self respect and feel good about each other.

For example, if you want to have a Harmonious relationship with your spouse, telling them by text that you didn't like the dinner they made will likely not go over well. Instead, consider waiting until after dinner the next day when you're both together and relaxed to say something like "You're a great cook, yet I prefer chicken over beef. I'm not a big fan of the baked salmon you made last night". Hopefully more great, Harmonious dinners, without baked salmon, will follow.

What if your teenager didn't do their chores? You could yell at them that night when they walk in the door or send them an email that day telling them how disappointed you are. On the other hand, you could wait until after dinner when all is calm and ask them what happened. Maybe they have an excuse or maybe they don't. In either case, a nice conversation about how to do better next time could go a long way toward a Harmonious relationship.

Another issue with communication may occur when one family member is sharing their troubles with another family member. Depending on the person and situation, the one expressing their trouble may be looking for empathy, validation, and listening from the heart, not a logical solution or recommendation. This is where John Gray's *Men Are From Mars, Women Are From Venus* book can come in be helpful to understand how to best communicate with the opposite sex.

Just like trust, there are many books out there on communication. The bottom line is when good communication is occurring with family members, Harmonious music and Joy are more likely to follow.

Discover and Appreciate

Our family members are so much more than we are aware of. They have so many life experiences that we are unaware of and talents we have never seen. The more you truly get to know someone, the more you will discover and appreciate how unique and special they are.

As discussed earlier, Dianne Collins' book *Do You QuantumThink?* discusses "Listening from Not-Knowing", a technique that can be very helpful here too. To apply this you must first be committed to the conversation with no distractions: no TV, no smartphone, no nothing. You must be focused and truly want to connect with this person because you care about them and really want to listen to what they have to say.

The reason it is called Listening from Not-Knowing is that with our family we tend to think we've heard what they have had to say many times before. In fact, you might feel like you know what they will have to say before they open their mouth. This is where you need to commit to thinking that each time you talk to them, it is a new conversation. Again, a new conversation is one that you will listen to with focus, you will treat as important, and one where you don't know what the other will have to say. In doing so, you will be amazed by what you learn, where the conversation goes, what you share, and how the experience of listening is enhanced. Often times, people who we care about are telling us things that are important, but we simply don't hear them. By applying "Listening from not Knowing", you will enhance the opportunity to discover and appreciate the different instruments you can play together and the likelihood of making Harmonious music and living better lives together.

Get Together

Many people feel like they are too busy to get together. They have better things to do. The meeting better be important. However, not getting together can lead to missed opportunities to learn about each other and make beautiful music together.

Times together, whether they're with your family, work colleagues, teammates, or fellow musicians can play an important role in getting everyone to play in Harmony. Getting together provides an opportunity for people to share ideas, to get to know each other better, and to collaborate on what's best for the team. Spending time with each other helps everyone better understand and appreciate what everyone brings to and wants out of the group. It can also play an important role to align and synchronize how the members interact and make Harmonious music together.

In addition, when groups get together regularly, whether they are with your immediate family or at the office, people can save important group topics for these sessions because they know the forum exists for them to be shared. In some ways, you can think of regular group meetings as a sports practice. The regular set times to work out the kinks and to run new plays. You're practicing with each other consistently to ultimately make beautiful Harmonious music together.

Consciously getting together with the Intent to enhance the relationship can have a profound impact. For example, your spouse may consistently nag you about how you park the car or how you drive. It may really bother you every time they bring this up. You can snap at them every time they bring it up, which can lead to an argument. However, another approach is to discuss the issue at a specifically set up time, such as when the two of you next go out for a meal. By taking the immediate emotion out of the interaction, you can create the opportunity for a productive, relationship building conversation.

Get togethers, especially regularly scheduled ones, give members of the family opportunities to share ideas, maintain good relationships, get to know each other better and stay in sync. It may surprise you what you learn about others, how trust is increased, and how Harmonious music and Joy develop from these times together.

Diversity and Inclusion

Can you imagine going to a concert where every performer played the same instrument. Not much chance of beautiful, Harmonic music here. The best Harmonic music in life is often made when everyone doesn't play the same instrument, doesn't have the same opinion, doesn't look alike, and doesn't do the same thing. The most Harmonic music is made when everyone's diverse talents, skills, perspectives, demographics, interests, experiences, and more are allowed to flourish and come together.

On the surface, you may think all or many of your family or team are alike. However, when you dig deeper, you will see more of their gifts from G-d and understand how when each utilizes their own gifts that the Harmony can be that much better. This is much more than being tolerant of others' differences. This is about being excited about them and finding ways to include them in the Harmonic music. Celebrate and appreciate each other's differences and you can make beautiful life music together.

Different Places

When we are with our families, it is easy to relate to each other in the context of our role within the family. You may be the mother, father, wife, husband, sibling, child, boss, employee, or colleague. You could also be the coach, player, or teammate. The list goes on. The point is that when you only relate to each other from those roles, it is often hard to truly get to know the true G-d-given talents and gifts of the other people.

For example, a husband and wife may choose to go on a vacation without the children to a place they have never been before. If they go into it with a sense of adventure, curiosity, excitement, partnership, appreciation, and respect, they will likely learn more about how they handle challenges, enjoy new experiences, and make music together.

A business group may choose to do a community service activity such as helping at a local food bank. The boss and colleagues may see each other lead and cooperate in new ways, while the employees may gain a new appreciation for how the boss works with them as they all make Harmonious music together for a good cause.

This is why getting away to a different place that is not the natural habitat for these relationships can have a big impact on making music together. Whether it's the house, office, or field, consider getting away for a lunch or dinner at a restaurant, a community service activity, or even an out-of-town excursion. It is amazing what you may learn about family members when you escape from the normal surroundings of that family. You may find yourself in different conversations than usual, you may find opportunities to play different roles, and you hopefully will gain a deeper appreciation for the instruments you can play together to create more Harmony.

Family Harmony

Each member of your family is blessed with special gifts, talents, and perspectives. When they are truly appreciated, cultivated, and free to be shared, beautiful Harmony can be made with everyone. The family is then in a place to have consistent Joy.

Joy With Family

The good news about finding Joy with Family is that the same techniques that you've learned for finding Joy Within Yourself can be applied here. By seeing the G-dliness in your family members and understanding that circumstances do not control your relationships, you have the opportunity to create your own reality of these relationships. You can choose to be in the moment with them, you can apply Observer-created Reality by choosing to bring a positive interpretation to the very moment with them, and you can apply the Five Senses and other techniques. In doing so, you can experience more consistent Joy with your different family members, the most important people in your life.

FOCUS ON YOUR COMMUNITY

Joy to the World! What a tremendous concept.

For many, it may seem grandiose and too overwhelming to be a reality. However, as Margaret Meade said, "Never doubt that a small group of thoughtful committed citizens can change the world". When one understands and believes that each of us can play a role and that each of us playing our role can change the world, amazing results can happen. It starts with Joy within ourselves, it spreads when we have Joy with our family, and it happens when we and our family share this with others in our community and the world at large.

Each of us can play an important role in making the world a better place. As the Lubavitcher Rebbe, the famed Chabad rabbi, said "It's like dropping a stone into a pool of water and watching the concentric circles radiate to the shore. If you strengthen your connection to G-d and behave in a manner which reflects this connection, then those around will be impacted by example and they, in turn will influence others. Remember to focus on yourself first."

We define community as "any group of people with which you don't have a close relationship, like your family." There is no size limit, and this can include people in our neighborhood, employees in our company, players in our athletic league, citizens of a city or state, the United States of America, and even the entire world."

Peace within Community

Mother Teresa once said, "Peace begins with a smile". She also said, "If we don't have Peace, it is because we've forgotten that we all belong to each other". She was right. G-d created each of us to inhabit this planet together, not alone. We all belong to Him and each other together and should thus find ways to Peacefully coexist.

When we have Peace within our community, people don't hurt each other or bring each other down. While we may not always agree with each other, we keep the Peace by not being derogatory to others nor fighting when we disagree.

This is a tremendous goal. However, there are communities that are experiencing it today. At the same time, there also seems to be many that are not. The news, social media, politics, and religions are just some reasons Peace in communities and the world is challenging. We encourage you to read books, watch videos, and listen to educators to learn how you can have a positive impact. If every person on this planet would try to have a positive impact, we could actually have "Peace on Earth" one day.

As John Lennon sang, "Imagine all the people living life in Peace. You may say I'm a dreamer, but I'm not the only one. I hope someday you'll join us, and the world will be as one."

Harmony within Community

When we have Harmony within our community, there is a mutual respect and appreciation for people of all different types, backgrounds, religions, genders, and so much more. It is more than just tolerance. We remove the labels on people and knock down the barriers created by them. There is a feeling of inclusion and of being a part of something bigger than oneself. It is the recognition that we all interpret the world based on our individual upbringings, traditions, and beliefs, yet most interpretations are fine and acceptable, especially since we are all created by G-d.

If we can have Peace and Harmony within ourselves and within our families, then we can apply this to our local, national, and global communities too. Truly trying to bring together different groups in a community for the greater good, truly listening to the perspectives of others unlike you, and making kind gestures to others you don't normally mix with can bring about new relationships, understandings, and Harmony in a community. The expansion of Peace and Harmony throughout the world could change many peoples' lives for the better and significantly increase the Joy felt by many.

Joy Within Our Community

Just like Joy within ourselves and in our families, we all have the opportunity to impact the Joy within our communities. When we are feeling Joy regularly and with the ones most important to us, we can now apply the principles and techniques we have discussed to make real, everlasting, and material change to the communities in which we live and to the world at large.

It could start by meeting with community leaders and asking them to recognize the valuable differences that each brings to the table. It is also about finding common ground, appreciating the importance each part of a community plays in the success of the community as a whole, and trying some new approaches. Whether these people are leaders from different religious organizations, different cities, or different business units, it is amazing how much more Joy can be felt by all when we're all in it together. We strongly encourage you to utilize the principles and techniques in this book to obtain consistent Joy in your community and the world.

FOCUS ON YOUR ENVIRONMENT

Planet Earth is a paradise. Trees, flowers, birds, bees, water, fish, and all the other natural wonders are amazing. They surround us with beauty, provide sustenance for our health, and are integral to our lives.

At the same time, our fragile environment continues to go through change, and some of it very dramatic. Many of these changes are caused by us humans and others my mother nature. While we know certain animals and natural resources have lessened or become extinct, it is hard to understand all of what is changing and the long-term impacts.

The Peace, Harmony, and Joy approach can have a tremendous impact on our planet. We all know that our lives are interconnected with the surroundings. We encourage you to respect, take time to better understand, and thoroughly enjoy your environment.

FINAL THOUGHTS

G-d gave us all freedom of choice. He has given us every "Piece of the Puzzle" we need to have consistent Peace, Harmony, Joy in our lives. He has also created each of us with greatness within. It is up to us to choose to put the pieces together, utilize this greatness, and live a life full of Joy.

The Joyful feelings we all experienced as children and so many more times throughout our lives are there to be experienced every day within ourselves, with the people important to us, and with people we don't even know.

Wouldn't it be truly Joyous if we could solve world hunger, global warming, and outer space together. Those and more are all possible when we are in it together and each do our part. It can be easy and effortless to do this when it is approached the right way. We hope you experience the ultimate . . . Peace, Harmony, and Joy!

Special note from the Authors:

While we have identified an approach to more consistently have Peace, Harmony, and Joy in one's life, we don't profess to have all the answers and know that many of our points can and should be discussed in more depth. We look forward to hearing your thoughts, comments and questions at www.peaceharmonyjoy.org.

Peace, Harmony, Joy

NOTES

_____

_____

_____

_____

_____

_____

_____

_____

_____

_____

Peace, Harmony, Joy

NOTES

_____

_____

_____

_____

_____

_____

_____

_____

_____

_____

Peace, Harmony, Joy
NOTES

_____

_____

_____

_____

_____

_____

_____

_____

_____

_____

_____

Peace, Harmony, Joy
NOTES

_____

_____

_____

_____

_____

_____

_____

_____

_____

_____

_____

_____

_____

Peace, Harmony, Joy

NOTES

_____

_____

_____

_____

_____

_____

_____

_____

_____

_____

_____

Peace, Harmony, Joy
NOTES

_____

_____

_____

_____

_____

_____

_____

_____

_____

_____

_____

_____

_____

Peace, Harmony, Joy
NOTES

Peace, Harmony, Joy
NOTES

_____

_____

_____

_____

_____

_____

_____

_____

_____

_____

_____

Peace, Harmony, Joy
NOTES

_____

_____

_____

_____

_____

_____

_____

_____

_____

_____

_____

Made in the USA
Columbia, SC
05 May 2023

16126796R00076